Elizabeth Nicholson

The Home Manual

Or, the economical cook and house-book: hints on the daily duties of a housekeeper

Elizabeth Nicholson

The Home Manual

Or, the economical cook and house-book: hints on the daily duties of a housekeeper

ISBN/EAN: 9783744793261

Printed in Europe, USA, Canada, Australia, Japan

Cover: Foto ©Lupo / pixelio.de

More available books at **www.hansebooks.com**

THE HOME MANUAL;

OR, THE

ECONOMICAL COOK AND HOUSE-BOOK:

Hints on the Daily Duties of a Housekeeper.

COMPRISING

NEARLY FIVE HUNDRED RECEIPTS

FOR COOKING, PRESERVING, PICKLING, WASHING, IRONING, GARDENING, PLAIN AND FANCY NEEDLE-WORK, PUTTING UP OF WINTER STORES,

AND NUMEROUS OTHER RECEIPTS, USEFUL AND NEEDFUL IN EVERY WELL-REGULATED HOUSEHOLD.

BY ELIZABETH NICHOLSON.

Who sweeps a room as by Thy laws,
Makes that and the action fine.—HERBERT.

Fifth Edition, Revised and Enlarged.

PHILADELPHIA:
ASHMEAD & EVANS.
724 CHESTNUT STREET.
1865.

PREFACE.

"In the days of other years," when persons in the middle walks of life were in the habit of keeping but one "maid of all work," the daily thought of "what we shall eat," &c., was not only the province of the female head of the family, but her occupation also. That is, to a certain extent; on any extra occasion, or the arrival of an unexpected guest, her hands prepared the fitting dessert, or the evening refreshment. And ably and well did she perform the task. Flinging rules to the winds, her judgment, skill and experience, stood her in good stead. Now, we have fallen on other days. If, as C. M. Sedgewick says, "the division of labor is the perfection of the system," then in cities we have it, truly. And, in many cases, it is well. Mothers of rising families can command much more leisure for higher and nobler duties. The sciences, heretofore brought to bear only upon massive machinery, have descended to aid woman in the thousand details of her daily task-work. Philosophy and chemistry have come to our preparation and preservation of food. Instead of the cooking range, with its bushel of coal, to prepare our dinners, while the thermometer ranges at 90 degrees, we shall ere long forget, in our beautifully systematized gas cooking, that our houses were heated from the kitchen, through our protracted summers; just as we now forget, in our brilliantly lit rooms, the vexation of the astral.

Still, work does not do itself. We admit many a servant into our houses to find that profession is not possession. The author of this volume considered, that an inexpensive little book, [so inexpensive as to render the inconvenience of lending unnecessary,] would be acceptable. It will be found to contain none but tested receipts, adapted to every-day doings, given in as brief a manner as possible, yet adapted to the smallest capacity; as she intends it for a Kitchen Book. It contains very few receipts under each head adapted to great occasions, because, under our present system, hired waiters are expected and expect to have all under their supervision.

To the women of America, therefore, I commend this volume, confident that its purchase, perusal and use, will be found a true economy, enabling them to devote more time to works which will minister to a higher need.

E. N.

Philadelphia, 10th mo., 1855.

THE ECONOMICAL COOK BOOK.

BREAD.

THIS staff of life, on which we lean for *bodily* support *thrice every day*, should never be made but of the best materials,—our health and comfort depending much thereupon. *Many a confirmed dyspepsia has been induced by the habitual partaking of heavy, sour, or ill-baked bread:* owing, in some cases, to the ignorance or indifference of the maker and baker—in others, from the want of the best materials, and the use of a *poor* stove or range. If, however, the following rules are observed closely, a wholesome, beautiful Bread will be the result.

So very much depends upon the yeast for making good bread, that we insert several.

Yeast.—Take 1 handful good hops, put them in a little bag in 1 quart of water, to boil. Pare 6 large potatoes and put in the water. When the latter are soft, pass them through a colander, (moistening the while with a little of the hot water.) Now, squeeze out the bag, and return the pulp made to the water, and let the whole be stirred, and just come to a boil. In this hot state pour it on sufficient flour to make a thinish batter. When *tepid*, add ½ pint yeast. This is fit for use in the *evening*, if made in the *morning*. Put it in a crock with a lid, in a cool place. [Those who are near a *baker's*, may save this work by *purchasing*, each baking day.]

Dry Yeast.—Boil 1 pint hops well in 1 quart water: strain it hot on 1 pint flour and table-spoonful of salt: stir it well, and cool : ½ pint yeast: let it rise; add as much Indian meal as will make a stiff dough. Roll it into rolls. When they are light, cut them up in thin cakes and dry them in the shade; turning them several times a day. Keep in a dry place : 2 cakes, soaked in tepid water an hour, and water all used, makes the *quantity* named, under *Bread*. I have eaten excellent bread made thus in summer. It is portable, and every way desirable for warm weather.

Hop Yeast.—1 quart water, 1 handful lively hops, boiled in a bag ¼ hour. Pour this scalding water over sufficient wheat flour to make a thin batter: add 1 table-spoonful salt; set it to rise. When light, add 1 tea-cup yeast. Keep in a covered crock, cool. [A little soda improves yeast when it is not very lively, put in when using the yeast.]

Wheat Bread.—Boil 1 quart milk : let it become coolish : then mix with it flour enough to make a very stiff batter : add ½ pint of the above-named Yeast, beat it very smooth, add 2 table-spoonfuls salt. Let it stand till light ; then knead it *well :* [the old saying of "bread is *poison* that is not kneaded," was put out as a frightener, I presume.] Let it rise. Mould and put it in pans.

Stand ½ hour. If milk is not convenient, water will do. The above quantity makes 4 medium sized loaves. If mush is desired, there may be a pint of it (when made) put in. *Better Bread than the above rules will show need not be*, if properly baked. The oven should be very *warm*, not very *hot*, and *slowly* getting *hotter* Bake 1 hour.

Bran Bread.—Take 1 lb. fresh Indian meal, 1 handful salt, and make into a thin mush. When tepid, mix in 1 wine glass yeast, 2 lbs. bran flour, [which may be had at the feed stores,] a table-spoonful of sugar or molasses; mix all together, and form a loaf *without kneading*. Bake in a pan ready greased, *longer* than the same quantity of wheat bread. Let it stand to rise in this greased pan, and bake. s. l.. [Rye Bread, ditto.]

Rye Bread.—Make a pot of mush with coarse yellow Indian meal—season it with salt to taste, and let it boil well for an hour, then stir in more Indian until it is quite stiff—let it cool until it is milk-warm, then add yeast enough to raise it, and knead rye flour into it, until it is a stiff dough—let it rise—when light, mould it into loaves. Let it stand till quite light again, and bake as other bread. Made into small cakes it is very good hot for breakfast.

Water Muffins.—Sift 1 quart of flour; add 1 tea-spoonful of salt; make a batter with tepid water, putting first into the flour 2 tea-spoonfuls of cream tartar; when just ready to bake, add 1 tea-spoonful of car. soda, dissolved. Bake on a griddle, in rings.

Butter.—*A good receipt.*—"In each pan of milk put enough of sour milk to make it very sour and thick in 36 hours: in moderate weather 2 or 3 table-spoonfuls will answer; in cold weather it should be kept in a room at summer heat. Skim it every night and morning, in a pot, and before putting it into the churn, scrape off the top with a knife, *as it will make the butter strong.* Work most of the buttermilk out—then salt it—then work it well with a cloth, till there is no more milk in it—print it—throw it in water a while, and set away in a cool place."

To Cure Butter that will keep for a length of time.—Reduce separately to a fine powder 2 lbs. of the best fine salt, 1 lb. of loaf-sugar and ½ lb. saltpetre. Sift these ingredients one above another, on a large sized sheet of paper, then mix them well together; keep this mixture covered up close in a nice jar, and placed in a dry closet.

When your butter is worked and salted in the usual way, and ready to put in the jars, use one ounce of this composition to every pound of butter; work it well into the mass.

Butter cured in this way (it is said), will keep good for several years. I have never kept it longer than from the fall until late in the spring: it was then very sweet and good.

It will not do to use for a month, because earlier, the salts will not be sufficiently blended with it. It should be kept in wooden vessels, or nice stone jars. Earthenware jars are not suitable for butter, as during the decomposition of the salts, they corrode the glazing, and the butter becomes rancid and unhealthy.—E. E. L.

Grafton Milk Biscuit.—Boil and grate 2 white potatoes; add 2 tea-spoonfuls of brown sugar; pour boiling water over these, enough to soften them. When tepid, add 1 small tea-cup of yeast; when light, warm 3 oz. of butter in 1 pint of milk, a little salt, and flour enough to make a stiff sponge—when risen work it on the board—put it back in the tray to rise again: when risen roll into cakes and let them stand half hour. Bake in a *quick oven*. *These Biscuit are perfect*.

M. A. B.'s Milk Biscuit.—Mix 1 pint milk with 6 oz. butter, ½ tea-cup pulverized sugar, 1 tea-spoonful salt, 1½ tea-cup yeast, and flour enough to make a sponge. Let it stand till perfectly light; knead it into a loaf, return to the tray and rise again. Then roll out the dough, cut it into small cakes, and stand ½ hour. Bake in a quick oven ¼ hour. Leave them in the pans till wanted for tea, to prevent the under-crust hardening. Yeast for these must be made the day previous—thus: Boil 4 large potatoes in 1 quart water; pour off the water and strain them through a colander; then add water enough to thin them, with 1 tea-spoonful salt and 1 table-spoonful brown sugar: let it cool and add nearly 1 tea-cup good yeast. This is a good yeast for bread.

Sally Lunn.—Three ounces melted butter, a half tea-cup of sugar, one beaten egg, yeast, a pint of milk alternately with the flour, making a batter too thick to pour. Put the mixture into two Turk's Heads, and keep them covered and warm, until light, then bake one hour.

Potato Rolls.—Boil 2 lbs. potatoes, pass through a colander, or mash them well; add 2 oz. butter and a pint milk; a little salt, 1 gill yeast, and as much flour as will make a soft dough; set them to rise; when light cut them in cakes; let them rise ½ hour, and bake. *Sweet* potatoes make beautiful biscuit, mixed as above.

French Rolls.—Boil 1 pint milk; cut up 2 oz. butter into it, add a little salt; when tepid, sift in 1 lb. flour, 1 egg beaten, 1 table-spoonful yeast; beat these well together; when risen, form into rolls, with as little handling as possible. Bake on tins.

Patent Flour.—Pulverize 6 lbs. wheat flour, mix 5 tea-spoonfuls dry carb. soda carefully through it; then 7 do. cream tartar, and 6 do. of salt. Incorporate these, and you have risen cakes at hand, to which add either milk or water, shortening or not, as suits, and you have several kinds of what is called soda cake. To this quantity of flour ¼ lb. butter would answer.

I find this flour good for crust of any kind: constant reference will be found in the volume to the use of it, in various ways.

C. B.'s Soda Cake.—Three pints flour; 3 tea-spoonfuls dry cream tar.; butter the size of a walnut; soda, 1 tea-spoonful dissolved in milk. Make a soft dough with milk and bake immediately ¼ hour.

Batter Cakes.—Muffins.—One quart milk; 4 eggs; dessert spoonful salt; 1 cup yeast. Beat the eggs well; add all the ingredients; make the batter very stiff by flour; grease muffin rings after the batter is light, and bake; fill the rings ½ full. Turn them over when brown below.

Flannel Cakes.—One quart milk; 4 eggs; 1 cup yeast; 1 dessert spoonful salt; flour enough for a thinish batter. Set to rise as above; bake like Buckwheat Cakes. Cakes ½ Indian and ½ wheat, are very nice. Quite good cakes may be made by leaving out the eggs.

Buckwheat Cakes.—One quart buckwheat meal; 1 handful Indian meal; 1 cup yeast; some warm water and salt. When ready to bake, ½ tea-spoonful soda, and 1 cream of tartar, lightens them. Extempore Buckwheat Cakes may be made by leaving out the yeast, and substituting 1 tea-spoonful soda; 2 cream of tartar.

Waffles.—Take two tea-cups hot hominy; 1 table-spoonful butter: when cold, add 1 tea-cup wheat flour, salt, as much milk as will make a stiff batter, and 3 eggs, beaten well. Mix, adding a mite of soda; do. cream of tartar. Bake in Waffle irons.

Quick Waffles.—One pint milk; 3 eggs, beaten; enough wheat flour to make a thick batter: add a table-spoonful butter melted, and a little salt, soda and cream of tartar.

Best Waffles.—One quart milk; ¼ lb. melted butter; 3 eggs; 2 large spoonfuls yeast: let it rise 4 hours. Serve them, when baked, with sugar and cinnamon.

Rice Waffles.—Beat 3 eggs; stir them into 1½ pints flour, adding by degrees 2 pints milk: add 1 pint boiled rice with 1 large spoonful butter, put in while the rice is hot. Salt, and add 2 large spoonfuls yeast.

As Waffles are rather slow baking, they will be nearly as good, if baked awhile before wanted, and put in the oven to keep warm.

Buttermilk Cakes.—Make a smooth batter of 1 quart buttermilk and flour: then add 2 large spoonfuls corn meal; 2 eggs, beaten; salt; 1 teaspoonful soda dissolved in milk; (no cream of tartar.) These are most excellent.

Mush, Mush Cakes, and Fried Mush.—Stir corn meal into boiling water till sufficiently thick. Add salt; keep stirring it to prevent its being lumpy. It should boil nearly 1 hour. Pour it out in pans, and when cold it makes a wholesome and good dessert, if sliced and fried. Eat it with sugar and cream, or butter and molasses.

Mush Cakes.—Take 1 quart cold mush, mix in it $\frac{1}{2}$ pint wheat flour, and a little butter or lard; make it in little cakes with your hands. Flour them and bake on a griddle as slab cake, or in the oven.

Corn Batter Cakes.—One quart milk; 3 eggs; salt, and as much sifted corn meal as will make a thin batter; beat well together, with 1 table-spoonful wheat flour; bake in small cakes, and serve hot.

Cornmeal Cake, in tins.—One quart meal; 1 pint boiling milk; 1 tea-spoonful salt; a teaspoonful soda; set it to rise in a warm place; beat 3 eggs and put in; a little cream of tartar. Bake in tins, and cut in squares for the table.

Cake, without Eggs.—Pour sufficient boiling water over stale bread to soften it; mash it through a colander, and add as much wheat flour as bread, and as much milk as will make it as thick as batter usually is; 1 tea-spoonful soda; 2 cream of tartar. Bake immediately.

BREAKFAST, ETC.

Chocolate.—Have 1 quart good milk boiling. Grate a piece of chocolate 3 inches square; mix it with a little cold milk, stir it in gradually, and boil ¼ hour.

Cocoa.—Put 1 tea-cup of cocoa shells into 1 qt. boiling water; let it boil ¼ hour; remove the oil, then add hot milk or cream, and sugar.

Tea.—The most approved method in this country for black tea, is to pour a small quantity of boiling water on the tea—let it stand on a hot stove (not to boil) for 20 minutes, then put it into the tea-pot intended for the table, and fill it up with boiling water. In pouring out black tea into the cup always put in the sugar first—then the cream—and the tea last. It alters the flavor entirely to add the sugar or cream afterwards.

Green tea, made in the same manner, but allowed to remain on the stove only 5 minutes instead of 20. In pouring out into the cup let each person add cream and sugar to suit themselves. Many persons omit cream—the Chinese never use it in any of their teas. They admire the scented tea,—but never use the colored poisons prepared for this and the English market.

There is a very neat article made for boiling tea. It consists of a small wire box, into which you put the black tea *dry*, then place it into the vessel in which tea is boiled; the advantage of this method is—no tea leaves can escape into the tea-cup, and you secure all the leaves compact.

Coffee.—This delicious and indispensable beverage is often either improperly roasted, improperly made, or, oftenest, a good article is not purchased.

Perhaps the surest method of always having a good cup of coffee, is to purchase a few pounds at a time of the very best *roasted* coffee, from reliable stores.

If this is not convenient, there will be found both economy and comfort in providing a bag of *old* Mocha, and having it most carefully *roasted*, not *burnt*, in one of the new "Coffee Roasters."

Boiling Coffee.—A large tea-cupful of unground coffee will be sufficient for 6 persons, unless they take it very strong, (which is injurious to health;) grind it, and put it in the tin pot, with $\frac{1}{2}$ a tea-cup of cold water, and the white of $\frac{1}{2}$ an egg; shake it till it is mixed; then pour boiling water on it, and let it stand close to the fire, and just come to a boil; stir it, and do not let it boil over; let it keep at boiling heat 5 or 10 minutes; then take it from the fire, and put in a $\frac{1}{2}$ tea-cup of water to settle it; let it stand 5 minutes, and pour it off. The "Old Dominion" Pot, combines *economy* with *good coffee*.

Boiled Eggs.—Put them in boiling water with a 3 minute glass in sight. If you wish only the white hardened, allow 3 minutes—5 and 8 for a hard boiled egg. Another, and more delicate way, and far more graceful to eat, is to break them into boiling water and let them boil 3 or 4 minutes; then take them up with a skimmer on a plate where is buttered toast. Put a little butter on the eggs. The most convenient way to have eggs done to your mind is, to purchase one of the "Extempore Cooks," an affair connected with the gas-burner over head. A nice way to poach eggs is to break them into muffin rings in water.

Omelet.—Break 8 or 10 eggs into a pan; add pepper, salt, and 1 spoonful cold water; beat them up to a stiff froth; meanwhile, put some butter in a frying pan, and when it nearly boils put in the eggs. As it fries, take up the edges, that all may be properly done. When cooked, double it; serve hot.

Baked Bread Omelet.—*Ingredients:* 6 oz. of stale bread, without hard crust; 5 eggs; $\frac{1}{2}$ oz. of parsley, and $\frac{1}{4}$ oz. of lemon thyme. *Instructions:* Soften the bread thoroughly in a dish, with a little boiling water, covering it over, and let it soak for an hour—then mash it up with a fork, picking out the hard pieces, and adding the parsley and lemon thyme, chopped fine, with salt and pepper, as seasoning. Beat the eggs well, mix them intimately with the other ingredients, and bake in a buttered dish, (buttered cold,) for about 40 minutes. Turn it out of the dish, garnished with parsley, and serve with brown sauce.

A Simpler Omelet.—Beat up 4 eggs; add 1 pint milk or less, season this; put butter in frying pan, when hot pour in the egg; cover the pan and let it steam a little while; then turn it up and up, and over into the dish, to serve.

Clam Fritters.—Strain them from the juice; chop the clams; put pepper and salt; add an egg or two; a little cream or milk; sift in flour enough to make them stick together. This is the most delicate way of cooking clams.

Corn Fritters.—Six ears of corn cut off the cob; salt; 3 eggs, beaten well separately; 2 tablespoonfuls patent flour. Fry brown.

Frizzled Beef, or Liver dried as Beef.—Put a piece of butter the size of an egg into a skillet; sliver up some beef and put in, turning nearly all the time, till done. Put the meat to one side of skillet, and put in a little cream, milk or water, for gravy.

Fried Ham.—This is good served in the same way; or, instead of cream, &c., 6 eggs broken into the gravy and served on the ham.

Salsify, or Oyster Plant.—Wash and scrape and grate it; season and make up into cakes; fry in lard; either use bread crumbs or not.

Egg Plant.—Cut it in slices an 8th of an inch or more; lay it 3 hours in salt and water; have a dressing of bread crumbs, egg with plenty of salt and pepper. Fry brown and serve hot.

Tomato Omelet.—Select 1 quart ripe tomatoes; pour boiling water over to remove the skin; chop them fine; put them into a saucepan without water, cover closely and simmer 1 hour; then add salt and cayenne, 1 large spoonful bread crumbs, and cover tightly; beat up 3 eggs to a stiff froth; have ready a heated pan with a piece of butter just large enough to grease it; stir the eggs into the tomatoes; beat all together, and pour it into the hot buttered pan; brown it on one side; fold it over and serve. This is nice with beef-steak.

Sweet Potatoes, left at dinner, make a delicate, wholesome relish, by placing them, sliced, into an oven to warm, and meanwhile heating and salting some cream or rich milk to pour over them. Serve hot.

A Relish.—Put bread crumbs into a saucepan with cream, salt and pepper; when the bread has absorbed the cream or milk, break in a few eggs and fry as Omelet.—C. B.

Omelette with Cheese.—Beat six eggs very light: add 2 table-spoonfuls cream, butter the size of a walnut, a little chopped parsley, pepper, salt, and 2 oz. grated cheese. Beat all well together, and pour into a pan in which a small piece of butter is melting: let it cook until of a light brown, then fold it over and dish for the table Shake the pan while the omelette is cooking.

Salt Shad.—For 6 shad take out the back bone. Mix 3 pints ground Ashton salt; 1 oz. saltpetre, sufficient molasses to make a paste to cover them. Let them lie 24 hours, then use, for broiling or smoking.

Beefsteak.—Choose the tenderest part of beef, an inch thick, broil it over good coals, covered with a plate; have butter, salt, pepper, and a little water in a dish; when you turn the beef, dip it in this; be careful to have as much of the juice as you can. When done, put it in a warm dish and pour the basting over. Some like beef fried better.

Sausages.—To 10 lbs. finely-chopped pork, put 4 oz. salt (scant), 2 oz. pepper, good weight, 1 table-spoonful ground cloves, and 1 oz. sage.

Scrapple.—Take a pig's haslet and as much offal lean and fat pork as you wish, to make scrapple; boil them well together in a small quantity of water until they are tender; chop them fine, after taking them out of the liquor; season, as sausage: then skim off the fat that has arisen where the meat was boiled, to make all soft, throw away the rest of water, and put this altogether in the pot; thickening it with $\frac{1}{2}$ buckwheat and $\frac{1}{2}$ Indian. Let it boil up, then pour out in pans to cool. Slice and fry it in sausage-fat, after the sausage is done.

Souse.—Boil the feet till the bones come out easily, and pick out all the bones. Pack them in a pan with pepper and salt, and cover it with vinegar or not, as you choose. Fry in lard for dinner.

Head-Cheese.—Boil in salted water the ears, skin, and feet of pigs till the meat drops off. Chop like sausage; season with pepper, salt, cloves, and herbs; mix all together; put it under pressure to cool. Cut in slices for the table, cold.

To Broil Tomatoes for Breakfast.—Take large round tomatoes, wash and wipe them, and put them on the gridiron over lively coals—the stem side down; when this is brown, turn them and let them cook till quite hot through; place them on a hot dish and send them quickly to table, where each one may season for himself with pepper, salt, and butter.

To Bake Tomatoes for Breakfast.— Season them with pepper and salt; flour and bake them in a stove, in a deep plate with a little butter over them.

FISH.

To Stew a Rock Fish.—Rub the fish with salt and pepper, and a little cayenne on the inside; put it in an oval stew-pan. To a fish that weighs 6 lbs., put a pint of water; when it is about half done, season it well with salt and pepper, and a little mace or cloves; rub $\frac{1}{4}$ lb. butter in $\frac{1}{2}$ tea-cup of flour, with a little parsley and thyme; stir this in with a pint of oysters. Serve it with the gravy in the dish. A large fish should be allowed an hour, small ones half an hour.

To Broil Shad.—Soak a salt shad a day or night previous to cooking; it is best to drain an hour before you put it to the fire; if it hangs long exposed to the air, it loses its flavour; grease the gridiron to keep it from sticking; have good coals, and put the inside down first. Fresh shad is better to be sprinkled with salt an hour before it is put to broil; put a plate over the top to keep the heat in. In broiling shad or other fresh fish you should dust them with corn meal before you put them down.

To Bake a Fresh Shad.—Make a stuffing of bread, butter, salt, pepper and parsley; fill a large shad with this, and bake it in a stove or oven.

To Fry Fresh Fish.—Have the fish well scalded, washed and drained; cut slits in the sides of each; season them with salt and pepper, and roll them in corn flour; have in your frying-pan hot lard or bacon drippings; dip them in egg before rolling them in corn flour, to keep them from breaking.

To Boil Salt Shad, Mackerel or Herring.—Wash the fish from the pickle; put it in a frying-pan; cover it with water, and let it boil 15 minutes; take it up and drain it between two plates; put a little butter over, and send it hot to the table: or, after boiling, you can flour, and fry it in drippings of any kind.

To Boil Salt Salmon.—Let salmon soak over night, and boil it slowly for 2 hours; eat it with drawn butter. To pickle salmon after it has been boiled, heat vinegar scalding hot, with whole peppers and cloves; cut the fish in small square pieces; put it in a jar, and pour the vinegar over. Shad may be done in the same way.

To Boil Fresh Fish.—After being well cleaned, rub the fish with salt, and pin it in a towel; put it in a pot of boiling water, and keep it boiling fast;—a large fish will take from $\frac{1}{2}$ to $\frac{3}{4}$ of an hour—a small one from 15 to 20 minutes. A fat shad is very nice boiled, although rock and bass are preferred generally; when done, take it up on a fish-dish, and cover it with egg sauce or drawn butter and parsley. Pickled mushrooms and walnuts, and mushroom catsup, are good with boiled fish.

SOUPS.

THE delicate and proper blending of savours is the chief art of good soup-making. Be sure and skim the grease off the soup when it first boils, or it will not become clear. Throw in a little salt to bring up the scum. Remove all the grease. [This may be best done by boiling the soup the day previous, and then the grease all comes off in a cake. To do so is often more convenient if you have bones, &c., which may not keep uncooked.] 1 quart water to 1 lb. meat is a pretty good rule. If it boils away—soup should not boil hard—add boiling water. The water in which poultry, or fresh meat has been boiled, should be saved for gravies or soup next day. If you do not need it, the poor do. And in connection with this remark I would say it is much better for all families to "seek out" some worthy poor in their own neighbourhood, to whom all their food, not presentable again on their own tables, shall be sent before it has become fit for the slop.

Beef-shin Soup—Mutton and Veal Soup.—Crack the shin in several pieces, and wash it through 3 waters; put it into a pot of water 4 hours before dinner—when it begins to boil, take off the scum as it rises, and keep it covered; 1 hour before it is done skim off all the fat, and put in potatoes, 1 onion, 1 carrot—either beat up dumplings, as given below, or roll them out of pie-dough, or bread-dough, if you have it, and put in—a few minutes before dinner, stir in thickening enough, with parsley, thyme, pepper, and salt, and tomatoes, if in season. A shin will make a good dinner for a large family, and will do to warm over for the poor (if any left) next day. To eat pickles with it, or pour a little catsup or vinegar on your plate, is good. Soup made of mutton, veal, and lamb, does not require many vegetables—carrots and potatoes are best.

Okra Soup.—Take a shin of beef and put in 1 gallon water after an early breakfast, and let it boil till 12 o'clock; then cut up 1 onion, parsley, $\frac{1}{4}$ peck okra, and 1 quart tomatoes; let these boil until dinner time, say 2 o'clock. This is delicious soup.

Hashed Beef for second course.—The boiled beef will make a very good dish, by cutting the meat into small pieces; a little cloves, part of an onion, some of the soup fat with crumbs of bread over the top-adding; bake $\frac{1}{2}$ hour in a quick oven.

Chicken Soup.—Cut up the fowl; cut each joint, and let it boil 1 hour; then stir in thickening, pepper, salt, and parsley enough to season; put in a few dumplings (made as elsewhere directed); let it boil up $\frac{1}{4}$ hour, and serve.

Pea Soup.—Leave 1 pint peas in the pot with the water boiled in; make a thickening of flour, milk, and butter, season with salt, pepper, parsley, and thyme; boil 10 minutes, and serve. Children are fond of this.

Clam Soup.—Wash 50 small sand-clams very clean; put them in an iron pot—set it in a hot place and cover it up. When they become hot, the clams open; then take them from the shells. Put the clams aside in a pan, and pour the juice into a stew-pan; let it simmer 5 minutes, strain it, and rub 2 table-spoonfuls butter and 1 flour smoothly together; put the juice on to cook, and slowly add the flour and butter; stir it well together; add ½ tea-spoonful salt, ½ nutmeg, and 1 pint cream or milk; stir this well, let it simmer 10 minutes, chop up parsley, and add the clams. One boil-up finishes, as clams require very little cooking. If you use the large clams, they must be chopped.

Drop Dumplings for Soup.—Beat 1 egg, add 2 spoonfuls milk, salt—beat in flour to a thick batter, drop them in the soup and boil 20 minutes before serving.

A good dumpling may be made of "patent flour" mixed with the top of the soup into a batter.

Okra will improve any soup. It is well to purchase it, while in season, a little every market day; slice thin and dry on earthen plates about the fire.

Be sure to take only young ones. These can be put in boxes for winter use; putting in one handful for soup.

Portable Soup.—Boil down the meat to a thick jelly, season highly with spices; dry in the sun. Put it away out of the air, and to 1 inch square put one quart boiling water—vegetables added.

MEATS.

WHEN a joint of meat comes from market, it is well to cut it up at once. Separate your roasting piece. Cut up the part for steaks, and put away in your coolest place what is left to cook afterward. Take out the bones you mean to make a soup of, and boil them soon, as they will not keep as well as the meat.

It is impossible to say how long meat must be cooked—much depends on the fire; coal gives out more heat than wood; beside, persons differ in what meat *well done* means. Red meat, like beef, must be cooked *rarer* than *white* meat, as pork. A good way to find how much done it is, is to stick a skewer in near the bone: if blood follows it, it is not done. Gravy for roast meat is made by putting some browned flour in, also salt and pepper and boiling water.

In frying meat, lard is better than butter. Mutton and beef suet are good: when the lard seems hot, try it by throwing in a mite of bread.

When boiling meat or poultry, skim it often, or the meat will be dark: keep it boiling. Put fresh meat into boiling water, salt meat into cold; allow $\frac{1}{4}$ hour for every lb. meat.

In roasting poultry or birds, be careful to baste and turn often. The back, having little flesh, requires little cooking.

Boileau.—5 lbs. 2nd cut rump beef—take out the bone—put 1 tea-spoonful of cloves and allspice mixed, a little sweet basil cut fine; rub these well into the meat; roll it up in a cloth tightly, and tie it—put in the pot some water with 2 potatoes, 1 carrot, 1 onion. Stew 3 hours.

Beef A-la-mode.—To a piece of beef 10 lbs. take 6 blades of mace, 12 cloves, half nutmeg—pound them fine, then rub the spice well into the beef: after the beef has been rubbed with salt and saltpetre, for 12 hours, roast it.

Roast Beef.—A brisk fire, baste often, season

well with pepper and salt—dredge flour. 20 minutes for each lb.

Roast Veal.—If a fillet, take out the little bone; make a filling of bread, butter, sweet marjoram or parsley. Lay the flank round the lean part, putting filling between, and skewer and tie it round. Put filling where the bone was. Sprinkle over all with salt, pepper, and flour, and bake.

A Roast Pig.—Clean it again after coming from market. Cut out the eyes with a penknife, clean the ears, take out the tongue, singe off hairs, &c. Make a filling as above, adding sage and more pepper. Stuff the pig and sew it up. Roast $2\frac{1}{2}$ hours, watching to prevent burning; if in danger of this, put paper between it and the fire. Baste frequently with salt and water.

Gravy.—Boil the tongue, liver and feet with salt and pepper till they are tender, in water enough to cover them when they are done.

Just before dishing up, take out the liver, chop or mash it up, work some flour into a small piece butter, stir all in—put over fire again, and come to a boil; take it off and pour into a gravy tureen. For sauce—stewed or baked apples, boiled onions, &c.

Roast Turkey.—Cut off the tips of the wings, the neck, gizzard, liver and heart, and lay them aside for gravy. Wash it thoroughly; filling as for veal (given above). Cook it 2 or 3 hours.

Gravy.—Boil the neck, &c., tender, with salt, pepper, &c. Thicken with flour just before dinner. Chickens—the same. An hour generally cooks them. For sauce—cranberry sauce, currant jelly, oyster sauce, &c.

Boiled Turkey or Fowls.—Clean and wash your turkey, as above—stuff with bread, butter, &c., as above, and, if you have them, some oysters. Have the water boiling, with a little salt; put in the fowl, breast downwards. Skim the pot often. Do not let it boil till the skin breaks, as it is then disfigured. Oyster sauce.

Roast Mutton and Lamb.—If a shoulder or leg, stuff as veal, sprinkle also do., and cook. Serve with asparagus, peas, lettuce, beans, &c.

Pudding under Meat.—Take 6 table-spoonfuls patent flour, 1 tea-spoonful salt, 3 well-beaten eggs, and 1 pint milk; beat this to a stiff batter; put a dish beneath the meat, which is roasting, to catch the drippings; when well greased, pour in the batter, and when brown, and set, turn it. A pudding an inch thick requires 2 hours at a good fire. Eat as a dessert or not.

Broiled Chickens.—Take those that are young and tender, cut them down the back and breast bone—wash and dry them. Lay them flat and skewer them down; season with pepper and salt, and broil $\frac{1}{2}$ hour on hot coals. Stew the giblets in water enough to cover them. When done, mix flour and butter and a little parsley chopped fine, stir it in, and come to a boil. Take off—dish the chickens and pour the gravy over.

Fricassee.—Stew a large fowl in water, covered close, till tender—seasoning it with salt and pepper. Thicken the water with flour and butter—pour in some cream—boil and dish it.

To Boil a Ham.—A large ham should boil very slowly 3 or 4 hours; should be put in cold water, and kept covered during the process. A small ham will boil in 2 hours. Remove the skin and save it for the soap-fat crock. Save the water and skim it, when cold, for the same purpose.

To Bake a Ham.—Boil it $\frac{1}{4}$ hour for every lb.; then bake it in the same proportion. Serve hot.

Tomato Stew.—Take 8 lbs. plate-rib of beef, put it on to boil in 1 gallon water, with 12 tomatoes, the same of okras, 6 potatoes cut small, 2 carrots cut longwise, 2 onions; season it with salt and pepper; let it stew slowly 4 hours; skim all the fat off the gravy, and garnish the meat with the potatoes, carrots, and tomatoes. This is a cheap, good dish.

To Dress a Calf's Head.—Procure a large pelted head (that is, one having the skin on); let the butcher cut it open, and remove the nose and eyes. Wash it well through many waters, into which put some salt to bring out the blood—clean the head well, removing the swallow and other things. Let the brains remain in the head, and soak all night. The next day remove the brains and skin them—wrap them in a little cloth, by themselves, and the head in a towel (clean one), fastened up tightly. Let the head boil about 2 hours, and the brains about 1 or $\frac{3}{4}$ of an hour. When done, take it up, and remove all the bones, and take out the tongue, which you may put back in the water to keep hot. Season the meat well with pepper, salt, and sweet marjoram. Lay it on a dish and cover it with the skin—on the top of which put the yolk of a raw egg. Sprinkle dry crumbs of bread on the top of this, with some lumps of butter laid here and there—season the top of this well, and put it into the oven to brown for about 20 minutes. Make soup of the water.

To Dress the Brains of the above.—Take the brains while hot and mash them in a bowl, add pepper, salt, and butter—chop a hard-boiled egg fine, and mix with it, and set it to keep warm—then slice the tongue through the middle, and lay it on a small plate by itself, and garnish it with the brains laid neatly around it.

Force-meat Balls.—Chop 1 pound of lean veal, very fine, season it with pepper, salt and sweet marjoram—add a little flour to make them stick together—roll into balls the size of a hickory nut, and fry them brown.

Gravy for the Head.—Mix butter and flour together, and brown it—add pepper and salt —add some of the water in which the head was boiled to thin the gravy. Serve the head on a plate, and lay the force-meat balls around it with a little gravy.

Veal Cutlets.—Cut the veal in slices near an inch thick; wash, drain, and season it; beat up an egg, and have ready some pounded crackers or bread-crumbs; dip the slices first in the egg, and then in the bread, and fry them in hot lard; mix a gravy of flour and water, with salt, pepper, and parsley; when the veal is taken up, pour it in; let it boil a few minutes and pour it over the dish, and grate a little nutmeg over.—E. E. L.

To Roast a Goose.—Make a stuffing of bread, butter, salt, pepper, sage, thyme, and onions; it requires but little butter, as geese are generally fat; wash it well in salt and water, wipe it, and rub the inside with salt and pepper. A common-sized goose will roast in an hour, and a small one in less time; pour off nearly all the fat that drips from the goose, as it will make the gravy too rich. Make hash gravy of the giblets, the same as for turkey.

Ducks.—Wild ducks are generally cooked without stuffing; and for those that like them rare, 15 or 20 minutes will be long enough; for common ducks, a stuffing should be made the same as for a goose; they will roast in $\frac{1}{2}$ hour. Currant jelly and apple sauce should be eaten with ducks and geese.

Rabbits and Squirrels.—Rabbits and squirrels, or birds, may be fried as chickens, or stewed in a pot with a little water. If you make a pie of rabbits or squirrels, they should be stewed first to make them tender, and then made in the same way as chicken pie. Rabbits are very good cooked with chopped onions, in a pot with a little water, and thickening of milk and flour stirred in when they are nearly done. Squirrels make very good soup.

To Fry Ham.—Slice the ham, and if it is very salt, pour boiling water on it, and let it soak a while; then fry it with a small piece of lard; when done, dish it; mix together flour, milk, parsley, and pepper; let it boil, and pour it over the ham.

To Cook Pigeons.—Pigeons should be roasted about 15 minutes before a quick fire; as the meat is dry, they should have rich stuffing, and be basted with butter.

You may bake them in a Dutch oven, or stew them in a pot, with water enough to cover them, and some crumbs of bread or flour dusted over them; let them cook slowly $\frac{1}{2}$ hour; mix together flour and water, with salt, pepper, and parsley, to season, and a lump of butter; stir this in and let it boil up; put them in a deep dish and pour the gravy over. Pigeons make a very nice pie in the same way as chickens.—E. E. L.

SIDE DISHES.

Fried Oysters or Clams.—Beat up an egg and grate a cracker or two, sprinkle pepper on your oysters or clams, dip them one by one into the egg, then into the grated cracker. Fry in butter and lard in equal proportions. They take but a few minutes.

It is a good plan to drain the oysters on a towel a short time, before cooking.

Mutton Chops.—Cut the ribs, season them, have a dressing as for fried oysters, and broil or fry. Make gravy.

Fried Liver.—Liver should be cut across the grain; pour boiling water over it, drain and season with salt, pepper, and a little sage—flour each piece and fry a very short time, or it will be hard. Make gravy.

Meat Cakes.—Chop any kind of fresh, cold

meats, season—make a batter of patent flour; lay a spoonful on the greased griddle, then a spoonful of the chopped meat, and then one of batter. Turn when browned.

Scalloped Oysters.—Toast several pieces of bread brown, and butter them on both sides; take a baking-dish and put the toast round the sides, instead of a crust; pour your oysters into the dish, and season with salt, pepper, butter, and mace or cloves. Crumb bread on the top, and bake in a quick oven $\frac{1}{4}$ hour.

Another Way.—Grease well a baking-dish with butter, throw fine bread-crumbs about in it until they adhere on all sides—have a bowl of seasoned bread-crumbs ready, and lay oysters into the dish, so as to cover the bottom of it; then sprinkle crumbs over them and a small piece of butter—then another layer of oysters, covered in the same way with crumbs, until the dish is full—cover the last layer rather more thickly with crumbs, and lay several pieces of butter here and there over it; bake it until it is nicely brown—not too long, or the oysters will be hard.

N. B.—Do not drain the oysters, but lift them with a spoon out of their liquor.

Fried Halibut.—Have the slices seasoned some hours before frying, as it makes it less liable to break in turning. Prepare egg-crumbs, seasoned—dip it in, and fry brown. Turn over. Make a drawn-butter sauce for this.

Cold Meat Turnovers.—Make a little dough of patent flour; roll very thin in a circle, and put in like a turnover—cold meat chopped fine and seasoned with salt, pepper, catsup and sweet herbs: either fry in lard or bake in oven.

Croquetts.—Take a cold chicken, roast or broiled; mince it very fine, or it will not adhere—moisten it with a rich gravy—season with pepper, salt, and a little mace; make it up in small forms in a jelly-glass, done over with egg and fine bread-crumbs—fry slowly in lard or butter.—R.

Beef Croquetts.—Take cold roast-beef or veal; mince it fine; put an onion chopped fine, sweet marjoram, a little powdered cloves; moisten with the beef gravy, make it into balls like sausage; put the yelk of an egg over them; flour and fry them in lard.

Chicken Croquetts.—1 pair fowls weighing 10 lbs.; boil them—mince it, very fine indeed; add 1 pint cream, ½ lb. butter, salt and pepper to taste; shape them *oval* by a jelly-glass, as mould; boil in lard, and serve brown. I know nothing in this way so delicious.

To Bake a Ham.—Make a dressing of bread, &c., moistened with three eggs. Take a ham which has been cut, fill up the place, and cover the top with this dressing; bake ½ hour, and garnish with parsley. Eat hot.

Corn Oysters.—To 1 pint grated corn, 1 egg well beaten, 1 small tea-cup flour, ½ tea-cup butter, salt and pepper. Mix them well and fry brown; make them the size of an oyster.

VEGETABLES.

For cooking vegetables, always have your water boiling before you put them in, and keep them boiling till done—standing after they are done will injure their colour.

Potatoes.—The medium size potato boils in 20 minutes. They should have the water drawn off them directly they are done, and put in a hot place a few minutes to dry—*waiting* spoils them. When *old* and not very mealy, to peal and wring them in a napkin improves them much. When *new*, serve with cream and butter in the sauce-dish. Sweet potatoes take rather longer to boil than white. Old potatoes are made white and mealy by paring them 4 hours beforehand and laying them in cold water: drop them into boiling water; and the moment they are done, pour it off and let them stand in the steam awhile.

Asparagus.—Tie it in bunches, the tops all one way; put some salt in boiling water; put in the asparagus, and boil $\frac{1}{2}$ hour. Toast some bread, dip it in the water for an instant; take out the asparagus and put on the bread. Make drawn butter.

To Boil Rice.—Pick a pint of rice, wash it clean—put in three pints of boiling water: it should boil fast, and by the time the water evaporates, the rice will be sufficiently cooked; set it where it will keep hot, until you are ready to dish it.

Hominy.—Large hominy, after it is washed,

must be put to soak over night; if you wish to have it for dinner, put it to boil early in the morning, or it will not be done in time; eat it as a vegetable.

Small hominy will boil in an hour; it is very good at breakfast or supper, to eat with milk or butter, or to fry for dinner.

Both large and small hominy will keep good in a cool place several days. Be careful that the vessel it is cooked in, is perfectly clean, or it will darken the hominy.

To Fry Hominy.—Put a little lard in your frying-pan, and make it hot; mash and salt the hominy; put it in, and cover it over with a plate; let it cook slowly for $\frac{1}{2}$ hour, or longer if you like it very brown; when done, turn it out in a plate. If you do not like it fried, mash it well, with a little water, salt, and butter, and warm it in a frying-pan.

To Boil Green Corn.—Pick out ears near the same size, and have the water boiling when you put them in; $\frac{1}{2}$ hour is long enough for young corn; that which is old and hard will take an hour or more; if young corn is boiled too long, it becomes hard and indigestible.

To Fricassee Corn.—Cut green corn off the cob; put it in a pot, and just cover it with water; let it boil $\frac{1}{2}$ hour; mix a spoonful of flour with $\frac{1}{2}$ pint of rich milk, pepper, salt, parsley, thyme and a piece of butter; let it boil a few minutes, and take it up in a deep dish. Corn will do to cook in this way when too old to boil on the cob.

String Beans.—String beans, if boiled in salt and water, will require fully 2 hours; but if boiled in a net, in a pot with bacon, they will not take so long; if they are cooked in the same pot with cabbage, it will injure the flavour. It is a good way to boil a very small piece of pork or bacon, or a ham-bone in the pot with beans; when they are done, season them with cream, butter, salt, and pepper.

Lima Beans.—Shell them, and wash them in cold water; let them boil about an hour; when done, dip them from the water, and season with salt, pepper, cream or butter; keep them hot till they are sent to table.

Dried Lima beans should be soaked over night, and boiled 2 hours or longer, if they are not soft.

Peas.—Early peas require about $\frac{1}{2}$ hour to boil, and the later kinds rather longer; the water should boil when they are put in; when they are tough and yellow, they may be made tender and green, by putting in a little pearl-ash, or ashes tied up in a rag, just before they are taken up; this will tender all green vegetables, but do not put too much;—when done, dip them out; drain and season them with butter, pepper, and salt; put a bunch of parsley in the middle of the dish.

Cold Slaw.—Cut hard white cabbage across the leaves, and put it in a deep plate; scald 2 large spoonfuls of vinegar with a piece of butter, some pepper and salt; pour this over the slaw; have an egg boiled hard; chop it fine, and spread it over the top. Some persons like it heated in a pan with vinegar and water, and the yelk of a raw egg mixed through it.

Cauliflowers, &c.—Have a pot with half milk, and the rest water; when this boils, put in the cauliflowers, and let them boil till tender; put in some salt just before you take them up; have ready drawn butter and parsley, to pour over them, or a sauce of cream and butter. Good heads of yellow Savoy cabbage, cooked in this way, resemble cauliflowers. Brocoli is a delightful vegetable, and may be cooked in the same manner.

To Boil Cabbage.—In summer, you should allow a large head of cabbage an hour to boil, but when it has been tendered by the frost, it will boil in half that time. Most persons prefer cabbage boiled with ham; the pot should be well skimmed before it goes in, or the grease will penetrate the cabbage, and make it unwholesome; take it up before it boils to pieces. It is very good boiled with corned beef or pork, or with milk and water, with a little salt added. Some like it with a little salæratus thrown in while boiling, as that tenders it and makes it of a more lively green.

Parsnips.—Scrape and split them, and boil until quite soft, either in salt and water, or with meat; they are very good served up in this way, with plenty of butter. They may, when boiled, either be baked with a few slices of salt meat, and require no seasoning but pepper, or made into small round cakes, seasoned with butter, pepper, and salt, and fried.

Carrots.—Carrots should be scraped, and boiled till soft in plenty of water; when they are done, take them up, and slice them thin; season them with salt, pepper, and butter. They are suitable to eat with boiled meat or fowls.

Turnips.—Pare and quarter the turnips, and put them in a pot of clear water, or with fresh meat; boil them ½ hour; drain, and season them with butter, pepper, and salt; mash them.

Onions.—After they are peeled, boil them in milk and water; if small, they will cook in ½ hour; when they are done, pour off the water; put in cream, butter, and salt, and let them stew a few minutes. Small onions are much better for cooking, as they are not so strong.

Beets.—Wash the beets; cut the tops off, and put them in boiling water; the early turnip beet is best for summer, and will boil in less than an hour; the long winter beet should be boiled 2 hours;—when they are done, drop them in cold water for a minute; peel and slice them; season with butter, pepper, and salt; send them hot to table.

To pickle beets, put them in a jar after they have been boiled; fill it up with weak vinegar; put in salt, cayenne and black pepper.

To Stew Tomatoes.—Wash and pour boiling water over them; peel off the skins, and cut them up; season them with pepper and salt; put in a lump of butter, and boil them in their own juice for ½ hour; stir in enough crumbs of bread to thicken them; let them cook slowly 10 minutes longer; be careful that the bread does not burn.

To Bake Tomatoes.—Take out the inside of large tomatoes, make a stuffing of bread, butter, pepper, salt and an egg; fill them with this, and set them in a deep pie-plate; let them bake slowly ½ hour.

Tomatoes.—If you wish to bake tomatoes in the oven with bread, pour boiling water on, and skin them; cut them in small pieces; season with salt and pepper, and put them in a pan with crumbs of bread and butter; cover the pan with a plate, and bake ¾ of an hour; when done, mash them and take them out on a dish.

To Fry Tomatoes.—Slice them, season with pepper and salt, and fry in hot butter; if they are green, dip them in flour after being seasoned.

Tomato Omelet.—Pour boiling water on the tomatoes, skin and cut them fine; to 1 quart of this, put 2 chopped onions and a lump of butter the size of an egg; let them boil ½ hour, then mash them; put in grated bread, pepper, salt, and the yelks of 2 eggs.

Spinach.—Wash it well; put it into a pot and sprinkle salt over it: cover it close, and hang over the fire to stew—a very little water. Stir it. Poach a few eggs, slice and put over it, with drawn butter last.

Egg Plant.—Cut it in thin slices; let it soak in salt water (or put salt between the slices) for several hours: wipe the pieces dry, pepper then, dip each piece in an egg which has been beaten a little, then dip them in grated crackers; fry them in drippings, or ½ lard and ½ butter.

SAUCES.

Caper Sauce.—Put some capers in your butter-boat, and pour drawn butter over them. Nasturtions make almost as good a sauce as capers, and is prepared in the same way—a few of them pickled are put in a butter-boat, and drawn butter poured over them.

Oyster Sauce is made in the same manner as drawn butter, only putting the flour and butter into the oyster juice instead of water: either cut the oysters in two or not: season with mace, salt, and pepper.

Macaroni.—Lay as much macaroni as will fill a quart bowl in cold water; let it soak $\frac{1}{2}$ hour, then put it into a deep baking dish, add a pint of rich milk, $\frac{1}{4}$ lb. butter and a tea-spoonful of salt, cut in pieces; over the top grate hard old English or American cheese. Bake an hour—it should be brown as a loaf of bread, and served in the baking dish.—E. W. T.

Drawn Butter.—Put $\frac{1}{2}$ pint of water in a skillet, rub $\frac{1}{4}$ lb. butter in a large spoonful of flour; when the water boils, stir it in and let it boil a few minutes; season it with parsley, chopped fine.—E. E. L.

Stuffing or Dressing.—Stuffing for poultry is made of bread and butter, an egg, salt, pepper, chopped parsley or thyme, mixed together; if the bread is dry, it should have a little boiling water poured on it.—*Ib.*

Egg Sauce.—This is made as drawn butter,

with one or two eggs boiled hard and chopped into it, and a little salt.

Celery Sauce.—Take a large bunch of celery, cut it fine, and boil it till soft, in a pint of water; thicken it with butter and flour, and season it with salt, pepper and mace.

PICKLES AND CATSUP.

To insure good cider-vinegar, it is safest to purchase it of some farmer who is known to have a cider-press, as so much of the beautiful vinegar we see is made from *a weed*, which eats and destroys the pickles.

Cucumbers.—Procure the smallest size; lay them in a wash-tub of cold water 3 days, changing them into another tub and fresh water 3 times a day: then wipe them dry and put them in the jars with whole peppers, allspice, and mustard-seed, and a handful of salt to each jar. Boil the vinegar 3 days in succession, and pour over them hot, till quite covered.

Martinoes.—Gather them when you can run a pin-head into them, and, after wiping them, keep them 10 days in weak brine, changing it every other day. Then wipe them, and pour over boiling spiced vinegar. In 4 weeks they are ready for use.

Cauliflower.—Keep them 24 hours in strong brine; take them out and heat the brine, pouring it on scalding hot; let them stand till next day. Drain them and throw them into spiced vinegar.

Pepper Sauce.—Take 25 peppers without seeds; cut them pretty fine, then take more than double the quantity of cabbage, cut like slaw; 1 root horse-radish grated, 1 handful salt, a heaping table-spoonful of mustard-seed, and ground cloves do., allspice do., boil enough vinegar to cover it, and pour over boiling hot, mixing it well through.

Universal Pickle.—To 3 quarts vinegar, $\frac{1}{2}$ lb. salt, $\frac{1}{8}$ lb. ginger, $\frac{1}{2}$ oz. mace, 1 tea-spoonful cayenne pepper, 1 oz. mustard-seed; boil these with the vinegar, and when cold put into a jar You may put in whatever green fruit or vegetables you choose, from time to time.

Tomatoes.—To 1 gallon jar take 2 table-spoonfuls salt, 1 black pepper (whole), 1 cloves do., 1 of mustard, 1 red pepper the size of an egg; mix these together and sprinkle over them, layer by layer, in the jars; let them stand 3 or 4 days, and then pour over boiling vinegar.

India Pickle.—15 old cucumbers; pare, seed, and cut them in thin strips; spread them on a board, strewn thickly with salt; let them stand 12 hours; then expose them to the sun, turning until perfectly dry, avoiding the night air: wash them in vinegar; put a layer of mustard-seed, onions, a stick grated horse-radish. Simmer in 1 quart vinegar, $\frac{1}{4}$ oz. tumeric, $\frac{1}{2}$ oz. race ginger, (both tied in a bag) allspice whole, a few cloves and cinnamon. When cool, pour it over the cucumbers. Excellent, and improves by age.

To Pickle Mangoes.—Take Musk-melons at

a proper age, before they get too hard; make a slit in the sides, and take out the seeds with a tea-spoon; boil a pickle of ground alum salt, that will bear an egg, and let the melons lay in this a week; then make a new pickle, and let them lay in it another week; then wash them, and scald them in weak vinegar, or sour cider, with cabbage leaves around the kettle; put them in a jar, and put the vinegar and leaves in with them; leave them 2 days, then wipe them carefully, and to 2 dozen mangoes, have an ounce of mace, 1 of cloves, some nasturtions, small onions, scraped horse-radish, and mustard-seed sufficient to fill them; fill up the inside of each one, and tie them round with strings. Put them in your kettle with strong vinegar, and let them scald a few minutes; then put them in a wide-mouthed jar, and pour the vinegar over; have them covered close, and they will keep good for several years.—E. E. L.

English Walnuts.—Gather them when nearly full grown, but not too hard; pour boiling salt and water on them; let them be covered with it 9 days, changing it every 3d day; then take them out on dishes, and put them in the sun to blacken, turning them over; then put them in a jar and strew over them pepper, cloves, garlic, mustard-seed and scraped horse-radish; cover them with cold strong vinegar, and tie them up.

Onions.—Peel small white onions, and pour boiling milk and water over them; when cold, put them in a jar, and make a pickle of strong vinegar, a little mace, ginger, white mustard-seed, and horse-radish; boil it and pour over them.

If you want them to be white, do not put in black pepper or cloves.

Tomato Mustard.—Take 1 gallon unskinned tomatoes; let them simmer in 1 pint of sharp vinegar 4 hours; then strain them through a colander, and let them boil till quite thick; then put in 4 table-spoonfuls of salt, 1 of black pepper, 1 of mustard, $\frac{1}{2}$ one of allspice. Boil all together $\frac{1}{2}$ hour. Then to each quart of juice add $\frac{1}{2}$ pint of vinegar, and bottle for use in bottles where a spoon can be inserted.

Pickled Beans.—Procure young ones from the late crop; boil them in water, slightly salted, till tender; throw them in a colander with dish over to drain; when done dripping, lay them out on a dry cloth and wipe. Pour boiling vinegar, spiced, over them, and you have an excellent pickle. These are delicate for tea.

Tomato Catsup—Wash and boil 1 bushel tomatoes. When soft, pass the whole through a colander, mashing the mass till it has ceased to drip. There will be about 11 quarts of juice. Put this in a china-lined kettle, and add 4 table spoonsful salt, 2 do. allspice, 3 do. ground mustard, 1$\frac{1}{2}$ tea spoonful ground black pepper, 1 do. cayenne. Boil this 2 hours at least: if you wish it thick, 3 or 4 hours. Bottle, putting a little sweet oil on the top of each, to exclude air. Seal, and it is ready for use in 2 weeks—is better in two years.

To Pickle Green Tomatoes.—Slice 1 peck green tomatoes; take 1 gallon vinegar, 6 table-spoonfuls whole cloves, 4 of allspice, 2 of salt, 1 of mace, 1 of cayenne pepper; boil the vinegar and spices 10 minutes; put in the tomatoes and boil all together $\frac{1}{4}$ hour longer; when cold put in jars. There is no nicer pickle.

SPICED SWEET PICKLES.

Cherries.—4 quarts cherries, 1 lb. sugar, 1 quart vinegar: boil some spice with the sugar and pour over hot.

Peaches.—Pare, stone and halve the fruit: put 9 lbs. peaches to 4 lbs. sugar, 1 pint vinegar: boil the peaches in water till tender, then put in vinegar and sugar, with a little whole allspice—½ hour, or till done.—R. B.

Pickled Plums.—4 quarts plums, 1 pint vinegar, 1 lb. sugar: boil the vinegar, spices and sugar together, and then put in plums, and boil awhile longer.

SALTING MEATS.

To Pickle Pork.—Take out all the ribs, and cut it in pieces of about 3 lbs. each; pack it in a tight barrel, and salt it well with coarse salt; boil a very strong pickle made of coarse salt, and when it is cold pour it over the meat, and put a weight on the top; if you wish pork to keep, do not put saltpetre in, as it injures the flavour.—E. E. L.

Pork pickle may be boiled over again and used. Keep a potato in it to test the strength. The "Burlington Herring," so famous, are cured in this way.

Beef.—To 100 lbs. beef take 6 gallons water, 6 lbs. salt, 4 oz. saltpetre, 1¼ lbs. brown sugar: the beef to remain in 11 days, then hang to dry.

Pour this brine over cold. Better dried beef than this makes, need not be. There is no real need of smoking dried beef. Tongues are nice salted in this way.

Dried Liver.—Engage a butcher to bring a whole fresh liver, put it in a pickle made as above, let it be in about 2 weeks, hang to dry. It is to be frizzled like beef.

Hams.—Take as much water as will cover your hams; salt enough to bear an egg, so that the egg will show above the pickle as large as a shilling, 1½ table-spoons of saltpetre for each ham, and molasses enough to make it the colour of cider or of good molasses and water: let them lay in pickle 6 weeks. Do not pack them too tight; keep them well covered with pickle, and remove all scum. Take them out and hang to dry. When dry outside commence smoking: a light mahogany colour is best, and bag before the flies come. Hickory or apple-tree chips are best for smoking. The above are superior to the mode of dry salting and rubbing, as practised by some; also less trouble, and making a more juicy and highly flavoured ham.—S. P. N.

The following is the method of curing Hams, which took the first Premium of the Maryland Agricultural Society, in 1854: To each green ham of 18 lbs. 1 dessert-spoonful saltpetre, and ¼ lb. brown sugar, applied to the fleshy side of the ham and about the hock: cover the fleshy side with fine salt, an inch thick, and pack away in tubs: to remain from 3 to 6 weeks, according to size. Before smoking rub off any salt that may remain on the ham, and cover well with ground black pepper, particularly about the bone and hock. Hang up and drain for 2 weeks. Smoke with green wood 8 weeks, or till the rind is a light chestnut colour. Pepper prevents the fly.

TEA RELISHES.

Chicken Salad.—Take a pair of fowls: boil them (saving the water for soup next day); when entirely cold remove all the skin and fat, and disjoint them; cut the meat from the bones in very small pieces, not exceeding an inch; wash and split 2 large heads of celery, and cut the white part into pieces an inch long, and having mixed the chicken and celery together, put them in a deep China dish, cover and set it away. Just before the salad is to be eaten the dressing is to be put on, which is thus made: Take the yelks of 8 hard-boiled eggs, put them into a flat dish, and mash them to a paste with the back of a spoon: add to the egg a tea-spoonful fine salt, do. cayenne pepper, ½ gill made mustard, 1½ wine-glass French vinegar, and 2 wine-glasses sweet oil; then add the yelk of 1 raw egg, well beaten, or 1 table-spoonful cream; mix all these ingredients thoroughly, stirring them a long time, till quite smooth. After you pour it on the chicken and celery, mix the whole well together. (Melted butter will do for oil.)

Clay's Chicken Salad.—To 2 pair large chickens 1½ bottles fresh sweet oil, 2½ table-spoonfuls mustard; begin by breaking the yelks of 3 raw eggs into a deep plate, add the mustard: mix it well round and round the dish: add about one tea-spoonful vinegar, then a very little oil at a time till all the oil is used: during all this time it must be long and well stirred, and always the same way. Have ready the yelks of 18 hard-boiled eggs, mix in very lightly into this about 1 tea-cup vinegar; let this second dressing be lightly stirred into the former, a spoonful at a time, then season the chickens with pepper and salt, add the celery; mix the dressing well through it, leaving enough to garnish the dish when served. The celery should be nicely cleaned, cut fine and put to soak in cold water till wanted, then turn on a cloth and wipe it quite dry.

To Stew Oysters.—Strain the liquor and put it on the fire in a nice vessel to simmer. To the liquor of 100 oysters take $\frac{1}{4}$ lb. butter and 2 table-spoonfuls flour; mash the flour into the butter till it is a smooth paste, then stir it into the liquor: season the whole with mace, salt and pepper. When the liquor simmers put in the oysters, and when the thin end *curls up* take them off the fire: they are done.—A. M. M.

To Pickle Oysters.—Take 150 oysters, put them in a nice vessel, with salt to your taste, over the fire. Allow the oysters to simmer, not boil: take them out and put them into a stone jar, leaving the liquor in the saucepan: add to it 1 pint good vinegar, a large tea-spoonful blades of mace, 36 whole cloves, do. whole pepper. Let it come to a boil, and when the oysters are cold pour the liquor over them.

Tongue, &c.—If the tongue is dry let it soak several hours before boiling it; slowly; if just out of pickle the water should boil when it goes in. A tongue-presser (which costs 75 cents) soon saves itself in making the small end go farther, and causing no waste.

Pickled Salmon.—Buy 2 lbs. salt salmon. Soak it all night in plenty of water. Put it on the fire in fresh, cold water. Let it simmer quarter of an hour. Have ready hot vinegar, seasoned with red pepper and cloves; put your fish in a stone jar and pour the boiling vinegar over. Cover close. When cold this is an acceptable relish.

Mock Lobster.—Quarter butter, 1 egg, boiled hard and chopped fine, mustard, salt and pepper, 3 table-spoonfuls vinegar. Have ready 1 lb. finely chopped veal or mutton, which has been cooked, and mix thoroughly the above ingredients.

Pickled Shad.—Clean them well and wipe them with a dry cloth, cut them in pieces of convenient size for the tea-table: then add as much salt, whole pepper, allspice, cloves and mace as you choose: season it properly, sprinkle the spice between each layer of shad in a new earthen or stone vessel, fill it up with vinegar; if strong cider vinegar it should have one-third water, and then tightly close the jar with dough, put it in the oven of a baker after the bread has come out, at noon, and let it stand till 10 o'clock, at eve; do not open it till cool through; bruise the spices, but not grind them.

CAKES.

The cost of Cake is so much lessened by being home-made, that it is a saving of time to make such as will keep awhile, by the plentiful use of good butter and eggs. The richest cake costs never more than 13 cents per lb., even when made at a time when butter and eggs are dearest. Besides, it is pleasant to feel assured of one's own skill in the matter, as we are liable to be called upon to exercise it at times and in places where money cannot purchase so good an article. There are few fancy cakes given, because there is no economy in making these at home.

Weights and Measures.—It is well to ascertain how much in weight certain cups and bowls hold, and keep them for that purpose. One quart sifted flour, or sifted loaf sugar, or softened butter, each weigh about 1 lb. A pint equals 8 ozs.; $\frac{1}{2}$ pint 4 oz.; 1 gill 2 oz. A quart of brown sugar or of Indian meal, equals 12 oz. of the same. One large spoonful flour, loaf sugar or melted butter, equals $\frac{1}{4}$ oz. of the same, a little heaped; 4 spoonfuls 1 oz. A medium sized tea-spoon holds 60 drops of water; 10 eggs weigh 1 lb.

Mountain Gingerbread.—6 cups flour, 2 do. butter, 2 do. sugar, 2 do. molasses, 4 eggs, 1 tea-cup ginger, 1 tea-spoonful soda, 2 tartaric acid. This is a batter, and if baked in a Turk's Head or bread pan, keeps a long time, and is very nice.

Ginger Nuts.—1$\frac{1}{2}$ lbs. flour, 1 pint molasses, $\frac{1}{2}$ lb. butter, $\frac{1}{2}$ oz. ginger, $\frac{1}{2}$ oz. of cinnamon and allspice mixed, 1 tea-spoonful ground cloves, ½ tea-spoonful soda, 1 cream of tartar.

Hard Gingerbread.—2 lbs. flour, ½ lb. butter, 1 pint molasses, ¼ lb. sugar, 1 oz. ginger, ½ tea-spoonful soda, 1 tea-spoonful cream of tartar.

Lady Cake.—½ lb. butter, ¾ sugar, whites of 16 eggs, 40 drops essence of bitter almonds, ½ gill rose water, 3 lbs. flour. Mix as pound cake.

Tea Biscuit.—1½ lbs. flour, ¾ sugar, ½ lb. butter, 1 tea-spoonful caroway seed, dissolve ½ tea-spoonful soda into a scant ½ pint tepid milk. This makes a dough, which roll in thickish cakes, and bake in a quick oven.

Jumbles.—Weigh ½ lb. butter, ¾ lbs. flour, ½ lb. white powdered sugar; put by a little of the sugar to roll them in. Beat 2 eggs well, add a little nutmeg. This must be made into a soft dough. Do not roll it on the paste-board, but break off pieces of dough the size of a walnut, and make into rings; lay them on tins to bake, an inch apart, as it rises and spreads. A moderate oven. These Jumbles are very delicate; will keep a long time, and are a decided improvement on the old method.

Golden Cake.—½ lb. flour, ½ lb. sugar, 6 oz. butter, yelks of 7 eggs, yellow of 1 lemon and juice. Beat butter and sugar together, and add yelks, lemon, flour, ½ tea-spoonful soda, 1 cream tartar. Bake in flat pans, and ice it while warm, if possible.

Silver Cake.—½ lb. flour, ½ lb. sugar, ¼ lb. butter, whites of 7 eggs, a little almond or peach water. Ice as above. These 2 cakes can be best made at the same time—are but little more trouble than one, and, cut in squares in a silver cake basket, make a pretty appearance.

Poor Man's Cake.—2 cups flour, 1 cream, 1 of sugar, 1 egg, 1 tea-spoonful soda, 2 cream tartar: the latter dry.

Cocoanut Pound Cake.—3 cups flour, 1 do. butter, 2 do. sugar, whites of 6 eggs, ½ tea-spoonful soda, 1 cream tartar, 1 cup milk: grate 1 small cocoanut, and put in two-thirds of it last.

Prime Bread Cake.—2 tea-cups risen dough, ½ tea-cup sugar, ½ do. butter, 2 eggs, a few raisins. Mix these, and add ½ tea-spoonful soda and 1 cream tartar. Rise awhile, after putting in Turk's Head.

Buena Vista Buns.—½ lb. white sugar, ½ lb. butter, 4 eggs, ¾ lb. flour, nutmeg to taste, ½ tea-spoonful soda, 1 cream tartar, currants or not, as convenient.

Cocoanut Cakes.—Grate 1 cocoanut, mix the milk with it, sweeten to taste. Form into little balls, put on white paper, and stand in a warm place.

Burlington Buns.—Rub ½ lb. sugar and 6 oz. butter into 2 lbs. flour: add 1 gill baker's yeast and 1 pint of warmed milk. Let the dough be soft as possible to mould. Make this at 6 P. M. Let it rise in a warm place till 10, then mould it over. Next morning it will be light. Make into cakes and rise awhile. Bake 20 minutes.

Philadelphia Buns.—1 pint milk, 1 cup butter, 1 pint yeast, 3 cups sugar, 1 egg. Make a soft dough at night. Early in the morning add not quite ½ tea-spoonful soda, and 2 tea-spoonfuls ammonia. Now put in a little more flour, mould it well, and return it to rise. When light, make into cakes, and let them stand ½ hour, or till light enough, then bake them.

N. B.—Either of these two receipts, faithfully followed, will make Buns which cannot be excelled.

Sponge Cake.—6 eggs, same weight sugar, ½ weight of flour, ½ a lemon squeezed in, the whole of the lemon-skin grated. Beat the yellow to a froth, then add the sugar: when well-beaten add the white, (which must be very light,) then put in the juice, then grating, last flour, a tea-spoonful of salt.

Another way.—5 eggs, ½ lb. sugar, 6 oz. flour, (leaving out 2 table-spoonfuls.) Beat the whites of the eggs to a froth: add the sugar and unbeaten yelks alternately, leaving out 1 yelk: add flour last.

Cocoanut Jumbles.—Grate 1 large cocoanut; rub ½ lb. butter with ½ lb. sugar, 1 lb. sifted flour, and wet it with 3 eggs, beaten, and a little rose-water: add by degrees the nut, so as to make a stiff dough: bake in a quick oven from 5 to 10 minutes. 52

Grafton Cake.—1 pint flour, ½ pint sugar, 1 table-spoonful butter, 2 tea-spoonfuls cream tartar, 1 soda, 1 egg. Make a batter of milk mixed, until quite thin. This is the best cake for the materials used in the whole collection.

Albany Cake.—Cream, 1 lb. sugar, and ½ lb. butter: take 3 eggs well-beaten, 1 tea-spoonful soda, do. cream tartar; add 1½ lbs. sifted flour. This is a dough.

Pound Cake.—1 lb. sugar, 1 lb. butter, 10

eggs, 1 nutmeg grated, 1¼ lbs. flour, 1 wine-glass rose-water; cream the butter and sugar. (I put the butter and sugar into a stove-oven till it becomes a little melted,) beat it some and add, by degrees, the ingredients named,—1st the yelks, well beaten, nutmeg, rose-water, whites, lastly flour. Make this now very smooth, put in ½ tea-spoonful soda, and 1 do. cream tartar; the latter dry.

I always bake such cake in a " Turk's turban," to secure lightness.

Baking is a nice point. The oven must be warm, and getting warmer, not hot to be cooled. If the latter, it is sure to be heavy, the cake browning rapidly prevents the inner part rising.

Cup Cake.—Cream, ½ cup butter and 4 cups sugar together; stir in 5 well-beaten eggs; dissolve 1 tea-spoonful soda in a cup of milk or cream; nutmeg, 6 cups flour, a tea-spoonful cream tartar, dry.

Black Cake.—1 lb. butter, 1 do. sugar, beaten to a cream; stir in 12 eggs beaten well; sift in 1 lb. flour, add 3 lbs. stoned raisins, 3 do. cleaned currants, 5 nutmegs, ½ oz. cinnamon, 1 tea-spoonful cloves, 1 lb. citron cut in small thin slices; these must be well mixed; baked in a moderate oven. This improves by keeping.

Queen Cake.—1 lb. flour, ¾ sugar, ½ do. butter, 4 eggs, nutmeg, ½ tea-spoonful soda, 1 do. cream tartar. Bake in small tins.

Crullers.—2¼ lbs. flour, rub in a piece of butter the size of a walnut, beat 3 eggs to a froth, and add 1 lb. sugar, nutmeg, 1 tea-spoonful soda, do. cr. tar. dissolved in Rose water. This makes a dough which is to be formed into twists, and fried in goose-drippings. These are cheap and excellent.

1, 2, 3, 4 Cake.—1 cup butter, 2 sugar, 3 flour, 4 eggs, nutmeg, 1 tea-spoonful soda, 2 cream tartar.

Kisses.—Take the whites of 4 eggs, beat them very lightly, and mix with them enough sifted sugar to make them very stiff; then drop on paper half the size you want them, and put them in a slow oven 20 minutes. Take them off the paper with a knife, and put 2 together. 4 eggs make a cake-basket full.

Jelly Cake.—Make a batter as for pound cake; bake it in cakes on a griddle, and while warm spread jelly between each layer. Trim with a knife.

A Good Cake without Eggs.—1 cup sugar, 1 butter, nutmeg, 1 cup milk, 2 oz. currants (or not), 1 tea-spoonful dry cream tartar, $\frac{1}{2}$ do. soda dissolved in milk, flour enough to make a batter.

Scotch Cake.—1 lb. brown sugar, 1 do. flour, $\frac{1}{2}$ lb. butter, 2 eggs, cinnamon. Roll very thin to bake.

Doughnuts.—1$\frac{1}{2}$ pints milk warmed, $\frac{3}{4}$ lb. sugar, $\frac{1}{4}$ lb. butter, and 1 nutmeg; make a sponge of these over night with flour, putting in 1 teacup of good yeast. Fry in lard. They are as good as possible.

Extempore Doughnuts.—1 tea-spoonful of soda, 2 cream tartar, 2 cups sugar, 1 pint milk, $\frac{1}{2}$ nutmeg, flour enough to make a soft dough.

Federal Cake.—1 lb. flour, 1 lb. sugar, ½ lb. butter, ¼ lb. currants, one wine glass brandy, or wine, or rose water; 2 eggs; nutmeg. This makes a dough, which must be rolled out in thickish cakes. These will keep three months. —E. C.

Iced Spanish Buns.—Mix 6 oz. butter with ½ lb. white sugar; add 1 tea-cup cream; beat 4 eggs separately, and put in. Have weighed ¾ lb sifted flour, 1 tea-cup Zante currants; add these. Dissolve ½ tea-spoonful car. soda in rose water; one tea-spoonful cream tartar to the same, but in another cup. Ice these and cut into squares.

Icing.—This elegant finish, is made by beating the whites of 2 eggs to a very stiff froth, and adding, little by little, fine pulverised sugar, till quite thick. Flavour with essence of Vanilla, or a mite of cream tartar. Lay it on with a broad knife, and smooth with another knife dipped in water. Set it in a cool oven with the door open, to dry. I prefer on the hearth under the oven. If you wish figures or flowers, make up 3 eggs, reserving a third till the cake has become dried after icing, then insert a clean new glass syringe into the remainder, and direct it as you choose over the iced cake. Dry again. It is said that ripe fruit may be laid on the icing when about half dry, with a very pretty effect, such as strawberries, &c.

Save a little icing out, dilute with rose-water, and put on when that first done is dry; makes it smooth and glossy. This is more trouble, however.

FLAVOURS.

Peach Kernels.—Crack the stones, take out and scald the kernel to take off the skin; put them into wine for use.

Rose Flavour.—Put rose leaves into wine for use.

PASTRY.

To make Pastry that will be entirely wholesome, mix 1 oz. car. soda with 7 drachms tartaric acid; put 1 tea-spoonful of this mixture in 2 lbs. flour. Put the mixture into a glass jar, with a closely fitting lid, after having incorporated it fully. It is then fit for use, and pie-crust should not be made without it.

Paste for Shells and Puddings.—Take 1 lb. flour, cooled and sifted, and 1 lb. butter: use no salt; make the flour into a stiff paste with very cold water, mixing it with a strong spoon: throw it out on the pie-board and roll very thin: cut the butter [which must be very cold] into small pieces and lay half of them on the paste: flatten each down by a quick pressure of the hand, dredge very much flour lightly over the whole surface, fold together lengthwise and crosswise, into a small lump: roll out again thinly, lay on the rest of the butter in the same way, sprinkle again with flour, fold together, and roll as thin as possible: dredge again, fold together, and roll into a wafer-like sheet, which, having dredged, fold lightly into a roll about 3 inches wide; cut the whole of this into squares, flatten each square with the rolling-pin, and cut out with a shell-cutter; having prepared 2 of these, take, with a small round cutter, a piece from the centre of one, and put it uppermost in a tin which will hold several. Bake 15 minutes in a very quick oven: watch them carefully, as much depends on baking. When properly made, these will rise to the height of 2 or 3 inches. The above quantity makes 12 shells, 5 inches in diameter.

A Plain Crust.—1 bowl lard, 1 do. water (scant), 3 do. flour: mix all well together, and roll out, using "patent flour" (if convenient). In the preparation of puddings baked in crust, the under part of the crust can be made by the plainer method, and $\frac{1}{2}$ lb. of the richer used as an edge.

Oyster Pie.—50 oysters: strain the liquor: line a dish with paste, take 2 hard-boiled eggs, chopped fine, 2 oz. butter: mix these with 1 slice dry bread crumbled fine; add pepper, salt and nutmeg to your taste; then to each layer of oysters sprinkle some of the mixture; it is best to reserve some of the oyster juice for gravy, which thicken and serve in a boat. Cover it with paste and bake.

Chicken Pie.—Cut up a chicken, and if old boil 15 minutes in water, which save, to put in the pie: make paste and put in the dish, cutting out the middle lay in the chicken, dust flour over and put in butter, pepper, and salt; cover them with the water, roll out the top crust quite thick, and close the pie round the edge: make an opening in the middle with a knife; let it bake an hour. If warmed over next day, pour off the gravy and warm separately; add it to the pie to serve.

Pot Pie.—Cut up 1 large chicken, grease a dinner pot with lard: roll out crust enough, [of "plain crust,"] to line it, cutting out the bottom. As you put in the pieces of chicken, strew in flour, salt, and pepper, a few pieces of the crust rolled thin, and a few potatoes: cover this with water, and put on it a covering of paste, with a slit in the middle. Let this cook slowly 2 hours; have hot water at hand, to add in case it be too dry. Veal, lamb, &c., may be made thus. Also, peach or apple pot pie.

Vol Au Vent.—Make up $\frac{1}{2}$ lb. flour into paste, roll out one-third of it oval shape. Take one of your dish covers and cut out two, leaving the bottom crust whole, but cutting the middle out of the second; lay them on a tin: cut out a third one, making a distinct line with a cover of smaller oval. Bake it in a quick oven, a light brown: take out with a knife this inner circle, fill in the centre with stewed oysters, fricasseed chicken or minced veal, hot. It is well to put in a napkin, to bake.

Mince Pies.—1 lb. finely-chopped roast beef, $\frac{1}{2}$ lb. suet do., $\frac{1}{4}$ peck apples do., 1 lb. raisins, $\frac{1}{4}$ lb. cleaned currants, 1 nutmeg, 2 table-spoonfuls ground cinnamon, 1 do. ground cloves, the juice of 2 lemons and rinds grated, mace, 1 lb. sugar, sweet cider to moisten it. Let this stand mixed, all night: when using, put in 2 oz. citron, cut in very thin strips.

Apple Pie.—Pare, core and wash $\frac{1}{2}$ peck apples. Put them in 4 pie plates with a little water. Make a crust, and cover them. While hot from the oven put in sugar, a small piece of butter, cream, or the yellow of an egg, stirred in. Turn out into a China plate.

Pie-Plant Pie.—Cut it up, skinning the stronger stalks, and strewing sugar over before the crust is put on. A little water. All juicy fruit like currants prepare in this way also. One lemon to 4 pies, grated all in, is good.

PUDDINGS, &c.

Apple Puddings, in crust.—1½ pint stewed apples, 1 tea-cup rich cream, ¼ lb. butter, 4 eggs, nutmeg, grated lemon skin, sugar to taste. Put in the butter while the apples are hot, the remainder when cool. Dried apples will do.

Pumpkin Puddings.—1 pint stewed pumpkin, [it comes now powdered,] 1 quart milk, 4 or 6 eggs, ¼ lb. butter, sugar and mace, nutmeg and grated lemon peel, or ginger, or other spice.

Potato Puddings.—¼ peck white ones, boiled. Beat them up: add ¾ butter, 1 pint cream, grate 3 lemons, all across, [take out seeds,] 8 eggs, 1 tea-spoonful soda; sugar to the taste.

Green Corn Pudding.—Grease a deep earthen baking dish with butter: grate with a coarse grater 2 dozen ears of corn, selecting such as are of equal ripeness: add tea-spoonful salt, table-spoonful white sugar, a quart of milk, and lastly, 2 eggs well-beaten: lay a piece of butter rather larger than an egg on top of all, put it into a slow oven, bake 4 hours; if the oven is too quick it will make the pudding curdle; when done it should be nicely brown all over, and the consistency of warm mush : good for tea or dinner : may be eaten with sugar, but a little butter is better.

Another way.—Grate corn from 12 ears of young corn : add ½ gill milk, 1 table-spoonful white sugar, 1 egg beaten. Mix all, and bake 1½ hours.

Flemish Pudding.—1 pint milk, 4 eggs, ½ pint flour, salt : boil ½ an hour.

Save-all Pudding.—Weigh out of your crock of dry bread ¼ lb. bread : put it on the stove with 1 pint milk to soften : let it remain 3 hours, then beat it up fine : cool awhile, and add 1 table-spoonful sugar, 2 do. Zante currants, 2 eggs beaten : pare, core and cut 2 apples and add : butter a "Turk's turban" and put it in : sprinkle 2 table-spoonfuls chopped suet on the top, and bake ¾ hour. Eat with butter and a little sugar

Cocoanut Puddings.—Grate the nuts, saving all the milk : to a pound of cocoanut add ¼ lb. butter, and ¾ lb. sugar; let the butter and sugar be mixed; the whites of 9 eggs [or the whole of 4] beaten well, 6 crackers, or same of dry bread rolled fine, wet with 1 wine-glass rose water, and all the milk of nuts : 3 nuts make 12 small puddings, or 1¼ lbs. of the grated nuts.

Cocoanut Custard.—1 nut grated into 1 pint milk, 3 eggs, sugar to taste, butter as large as a walnut, the outside of a lemon and nutmeg.

Soda Cracker Pudding.—4 soda crackers soaked in 3 tea-cups water, 2 lemons grated in, and 2 tea-cups sugar. These taste like apple pie.

Apple Custard.—Pare tart apples, core them with an an apple corer, put them in a deep dish with a small piece of butter, and 1 tea-spoonful sugar in the opening of each apple. Pour in water enough to cook them: when soft, cool them, and pour over an unbaked custard so as to cover them, and bake till custard is done.

Apple Meringue.—Pare, core and stew 10 tart apples, in a very little water: season as for a pie, and put it in a fruit pie dish, into a cool oven. Beat up, meanwhile, the whites of 4 eggs as you would for icing: piling it on the apple like rocks, or irregular, avoiding the edge of dish. Return it to a warm oven, and brown macaroni colour. Slip all out carefully, by aid of knife or spoon, into a China dish, and serve with cream, which if you have not, make a custard of the yellows, flavoured with essence of Vanilla, &c.

Custard may be used instead of apple; it may be a soft one, and in cups.

Rice Pudding.—Wash 3 heaping table-spoonfuls rice: put it into 1 quart milk, a pinch of salt, white sugar to taste, a little nutmeg and butter. Put it in the oven directly after breakfast, in a warmish oven: let it simmer, and when a brown skin begins to form stir it in. Do this 3 times. You will thus have a creamy pudding. Raisins or not.

Macaroon Pudding.—Boil 1 quart milk, dissolve the weight of 4 cents' worth Russian isinglass in as little water as possible: add it to the boiling milk. Roll 12 macaroons, (chocolate if you choose,) to a fine powder: stir it in the milk, and pour it into a mould. Eat cold, with cream.
—E. W. T.

Iced Apples.—Pare, core, and spice 10 apples of a large tart kind. Bake them till nearly done.

Put them away to get entirely cold : then prepare some icing as for Apple Meringue, and, first pouring off all the juice, lay the icing thickly on the tops and sides as much as you can. Return them to the oven to just harden and be set. Serve with cream. This is very beautiful, either for dessert or an evening.

Apple Tapioca.—Core some tart apples: fill up the opening with butter and sugar, strew some sugar around them. Put 1 dessert-spoonful dry Tapioca to each apple. Put water around, nearly up to the top of apples: bake, and serve as the above.

Apple Float.—Prepare 12 tart apples as for sauce: when cold, add 2 whites of eggs, beaten : then beat the whole till quite stiff. Have made previously a soft custard, with the 2 yelks. Put the apple on the custard.

Adelaide's Pudding.—Pare and core, and fill up with nutmeg, sugar and butter, 6 apples. Make a batter of 1 egg, patent flour, ½ pint milk, and pour round. A little salt in batter. [These varieties of apple dessert are healthful, cheap, easily made, and excellent.]

Cup Batter Pudding.—6 eggs, 6 table-spoonfuls flour, 1 pint milk, 1 tea-spoonful salt. Beat the yelks apart well, and mix them with the flour : then add the milk. Lastly, whip the white stiff, mix and bake at once, ½ hour.

Boiled Batter Pudding.—6 eggs, 1 quart milk, 12 table-spoonfuls sifted flour, (or more, if preferred,) 1 tea-spoon salt. Mix as other batter; have water boiling. Dip your bag into the hot water; take it out, and sift flour inside. Pour in the batter and tie it tightly, leaving room for the pudding to swell. Put it in now and boil 1½ hours. To be eaten hot with sauce No. 1 or 4. A pound of currants, or any fruit preferred: boil awhile longer for them, and turn over frequently, or the fruit will settle to one side.

A Bread Pudding.—1 quart milk, 4 eggs, ½ lb. dried currants, a few slices stale bread, 1 teaspoon salt. Bake in a quick oven ½ hour. Eat it with sauce No. 2 or 4. Another way is to put alternate slices of apple and bread, and bake.

Fritters, with Yeast.—Make a batter of 1 pint milk, and as much flour as will form it, 1 teaspoon salt, and 5 table-spoons yeast. Put this in a warm place 3 hours. Just before dinner beat up 1 egg well, and add. These fritters are quite wholesome, being light, and do not absorb much lard. Boil them in lard.

Delightful Pudding.—1 quart boiled milk, ¼ lb. mashed potatoes, ¼ lb. flour, a small piece butter, and when cold add 3 eggs, beaten. Bake ½ hour. Eat with sauce No. 2.

Cottage Pudding.—1 pint flour, ½ pint sugar, ¼ lb. butter, 2 eggs, ½ pint milk, 2 tea-spoonfuls cream tartar, 1 do. soda, a few currants or stoned raisins. Bake ½ hour in a Turk's turban. This is very good to put on at tea as a cake, if left at dinner. Sauce No. 2.

Stale Bread Fritters.—Make as the above-named fritters, substituting bread for flour. These are more tender.

Cold Custard.—To 1 quart milk, (sweetened with white sugar to taste,) add 3 table-spoonfuls wine, in which rennet has been placed. Pour it immediately into custard cups, and let it stand in a cool place several hours before dinner. Grate a little nutmeg over each, and eaten with cream, you have a dessert often more acceptable than a more elaborate and costly one. Put 1 calf's rennet, cut in strips, into 1 quart wine: let it remain a week, and use as directed.

Custard Pudding.—Beat the yelks of 4 eggs smooth, adding, (little by little,) 1 quart milk, scant. Sweeten to taste: a pinch of salt, slice stale bread very thin, spread butter over it, then nutmeg, and lay on the top. Bake till custard is thick. [Salt enriches any kind of custard or batter: put in 1 tea-spoonful to 2 quarts.]

Trifle.—Break rusk or sponge cake into a dish, pour a boiled custard over it, and put a syllabub over that. Garnished with jelly and flowers, this makes a handsome dessert.

Syllabub.—Make 1 quart rich cream very sweet, grate ½ nutmeg over it, put it into a China bowl, and milk a cow into it, that it may be very frothy.

Floating Island.—Take the whites of 3 eggs, beat them to a froth: put 4 spoonfuls any kind of jelly, or roast apple; beat them together till it becomes a substance that will heap on a spoon. Meanwhile, have made a boiled custard of 1½ pint milk to the 3 unused yelks. Put the island on, and pile up like rocks.

Another Way.—The whites of 8 eggs in a deep earthen bowl: add a small tea-cupful of currant jelly, beaten altogether until it forms a stiff froth in a cold place; (the eggs should be at least 2 days old, and very cold.) Pour cream into a glass bowl, and drop the island from a large spoon on to the surface of the cream.

Bird's Nest Pudding.—Make the foundation of the nest of blancmange, or calf's foot jelly, or prepared corn: rasp the skin of 3 lemons and preserve it; then lay it round and on the mange like the straw: take out the contents of 4 eggs through a small hole, and fill the shell with hot blancmange, or prepared corn; when cold, break off the shells and lay mange in the nest. A beautiful dessert.

Charlotte Russe.—1½ oz. isinglass dissolved in 1 pint water; let it simmer to ½ pint. Make a custard of 4 eggs to 1 pint milk; cool it; boil a vanilla bean in the milk, whip 1 qt. of cream to a froth, lay it on a sieve after it is whipped; stir the custard into the isinglass, then add the whipped cream, beat all together. Line a glass dish with sponge cake, and serve.

N. B.—This is a very beautiful dessert, and if you have no sponge cake, any stale cake will do; cut it in thin slices.

The whipped cream receipt will be found on page 67. Keep the cream in a cold place, after beating.

Tapioca Pudding.—2 oz. to 1 pint milk, softened in the oven, and when nearly cold add 3 eggs, and a little butter and sugar. Bake or boil 1 hour

Baked Indian Pudding.—Cut up ¼ lb. butter in 1 pint molasses, warm them till melted. Boil 1 quart milk, and pour over a pint corn meal, and stir in the molasses gradually: when cold, beat 6 eggs and stir them in: add the peel of a lemon, grated, or other spice: stir very hard, pour into a buttered dish, and bake 2 hours.—J. G.

Frozen Custard.—Make a custard as for a pudding. Let it boil: sweeten and flavour, then freeze it.

A. H.'s Custard.—Put into a milk boiler 1 quart milk: add a mite of salt: let it come to a boil: have 2 eggs whipped together, with sugar enough to sweeten the whole. When the milk is scalded, pour it by degrees upon the egg, stirring it the while: flavour with vanilla or almond, and pour it out in a basin, with a few pieces of thin bread and butter, or into custard cups: set these into a basin of hot water, and put into an oven. In a short time it will thicken into a delicate custard.

Blanc Mange of Carrigeen.—Wash ½ oz. Carrigeen moss; put it to boil in 2 quarts good milk; a little salt. While boiling, sweeten to taste, and flavor with vanilla; let it boil 10 minutes; then pour it into moulds, and eat with cream or soft custard. Gelatin B. M. is made by putting 1 package to the above; soaking it 20 minutes in cold water, previously.

Snow Fritters.—Take of light new-fallen snow, 3 table-spoonfuls for every egg you would otherwise use—that is, if you would wish the quantity that 3 eggs would make in the usual way, take 9 table-spoonfuls of snow, and stir in a quart of rich milk that has been setting in a very cold place, so that it will not melt the snow, and destroy its lightness; put in a tea-spoonful of salt, and enough wheat flour to make a stiff batter; have ready a frying-pan with boiling lard, and drop a spoonful in a place as with other fritters, and set the remainder in a cold place till the first are done. Eat them with wine sauce, or sugar, butter and cream, or any thing you fancy. Put in snow last.

Rice Flummery.—Rice that is ground coarse, in a hand-mill, is much better for making flummery than the flour you buy; put 3 pints of milk to boil, mix with water 1 tea-cup of ground rice, and stir it in the milk when it boils; while the milk is cold, put in it 2 dozen peach kernels, blanched, and rolled with a bottle; wet your moulds with cold cream or water; keep stirring the rice till it is thick, when pour it out in the moulds; just before dinner turn them out on dishes, have cream, sugar and nutmeg mixed, to eat with it.

Whipped Cream.—Take 1 pint rich cream, 1 tea-cup sifted sugar, essence of lemon or the grated rind, to taste; put this into a large pitcher, churn it with a whipped-cream churn, (which you may get at a tinman's for 25 cents,) until all of it comes to a froth: then place it with a spoon upon any mould dessert. This is very delicate and pretty, and will double the cream used.—A. P.

Sauces. No. 1.—Mix 1 tea-spoonful flour in 1 tea-cup water, with 2 spoonfuls sugar and 1 butter: stir this in ½ pint boiling water, let it boil a few minutes; when add 1 glass wine and nutmeg.

No. 2.—Beat equal quantities of butter and white sugar to a cream, grate nutmeg into it. Beat all well together, and put to harden before serving it.

No. 3.—Melt molasses, butter and vinegar together.

No. 4, Cream Sauce.—Boil ½ pint cream, thicken it very little, put in a lump of butter: sweeten to taste, and when cold add 1 glass wine, or a lemon rind and juice.

JELLIES.

Calf's Foot Jelly.—Clean 6 feet: put them on to boil in 2½ quarts water and ½ tea-spoonful salt: boil down one-half, strain it, and when cold scrape off all the fat, using a piece of silk paper last. Put it into a porcelain kettle, add sugar and wine to the taste, the rind of 2 lemons and juice, the whites of 4 eggs and shells: let it boil hard 20 minutes, without stirring; strain it through a flannel bag into moulds. It is more likely to turn out perfectly if made the day before used.

Tapioca Jelly.—Soak 3 table-spoonfuls pearl Tapioca in 1 quart water, several hours: put it in a saucepan with the same water, and let it boil slowly till clear and thick. Season with wine or lemon, and white sugar. Turn out in moulds.

Gelatine Jelly.—Take 3 oz. Gelatine, 2 quarts water, 1 pint wine, (or lemon juice enough to flavour,) 1½ lbs. white sugar, whites of 3 eggs and shells; boil 20 minutes, and pour as above.

Currant Jelly.—4 quarts ripe currants mashed in both hands, till nearly all are broken; squeeze out the stems and remove them. Put the pulp into a strong bag and squeeze very tightly, and there will be nearly 3 pints juice. Put 3 lbs. white sugar to this, and boil ½ hour.

Apple Jelly.—Slice whole apples, (cores, parings and all,) cook them with just water enough to cover them, till reduced to a soft pulp. Take the rind and juice of 4 lemons; strain this pulp, (not squeezing much or going over it twice,) add the lemons, measure pint for lb. white sugar; let it boil ½ hour, and turn into forms. Quince &c., the same way.

Rice Jelly.—Boil ¼ lb. whole rice with ½ lb. loaf sugar, in 1 quart water, till it becomes a glutinous mass. Strain off the jelly and let it cool, in moulds.

Quince Jelly.—Wash and wipe the quinces; cut them in small pieces, and take out the seeds carefully; have your kettle cleaned and half full of water; throw the quinces and seeds in till you get it full; cover them over, and let them boil till very soft; mash them well and strain them; to every pint of juice put a pound of sugar; clean the kettle again, pour in the juice and sugar, and let it boil till it forms a jelly; it should be put into tea-cups, if you want it to turn out whole, with brandy papers on the top, and pasted over. It is a nice jelly to use with whips or trifle.

Molasses Candy or Taffy.—Put a quart of good molasses (not sugar-house) in a Dutch oven or iron pot, having previously greased it with butter; let it boil very fast, stirring it all the time for 15 minutes; then put in a tea-cup of sugar and let it boil 15 minutes longer, stirring all the time; take a little out on a plate, and when it is brittle, pour it while hot into tin plates rubbed with butter; put it in a cold place and break it up when you want it for use; never put taffy in China or earthen plates, as they would probably be broken in taking it out. Some think it an improvement to add the kernels of black walnuts, nicely picked; put them in just as you take up the taffy and give it one stir; a tea-cup of kernels to a pint of molasses is a good proportion.

Quince Jam.—Grate quinces which have been pared, cored and halved: to 1 lb. quince, after grated, $\frac{3}{4}$ sugar: boil 20 minutes. This is very light coloured, and if put in moulds or bowls turns out well.

Blancmange in Eggs.—Have ready some egg-shells, which have been broken as little as possible; dissolve $\frac{1}{2}$ oz. gelatine in a very little warm water, and then stir in 1 pint good milk; sweeten and flavour it. Boil it $\frac{1}{4}$ hour, stirring frequently. Strain it, and put it into the egg-shells to cool. When congealed, have ready a China or glass dish of calves' feet jelly; break the shells from off the mange, cut them in half, scoop out a little of the middle, and insert some of the calves' feet jelly to imitate the yelk. These placed over the surface of the dish have a pretty birds'-nest look. Cream served with it is good, but not needful.

PRESERVES.

These are costly affairs in every way: not done without fatigue, time and patience—to say nothing of their unwholesomeness for some. We give a few.

Cocoanut Preserved.—Grate 1 nut, save the milk and put in; sweeten to taste with powdered loaf, and cook ¼ hour, stirring all the time to prevent burning. This is very pretty for puffs, but sickish.

Preserved Pine Apple.—Take lb. for lb. of sugar; boil the slices in water a few at a time, till clear. Then make a syrup with the water, and cook the apples 15 minutes in it. If the syrup is not slightly thick, boil it longer.

Grated Pine Apple.—Grate the apples whole, and take lb. for lb.; boil 20 minutes, stirring often.

Common Cherries.—Stone the light-coloured common cherries, and to every pound of fruit allow a pound of sugar, which boil up with the juice; after you have skimmed it throw in the cherries, and let them boil till the syrup is rich.

Cherries for common use.—Stone 12 lbs. of good cherries; allow ½ lb. of brown sugar to each pound of fruit, after it is stoned; let them cook slowly for 2 hours; examine them through the summer, and if they show any signs of fermentation set them in a brick oven, after the bread is done, or in a Dutch oven of hot water, which keep at boiling heat for an hour.

It is a good plan to know the weight of your preserving kettle, as you can then weigh the fruit in it, with a pair of steelyards.—LEA.

Gooseberries.—Take the large gooseberries, pick off the stems and blossoms, give them their weight in sugar; put them in the kettle alternately, with the sugar, and pour over them a pint of water to 4 lbs. of fruit; let them boil gently till the scum arises; when this is taken off, let them cook faster; when clear, take them up on dishes, and boil the syrup longer.

Peaches.—Have sweet, white clingstone peaches, pare and stone them; to each lb. take a pound of sugar made in a syrup, put the peaches in, and when they look clear take them up on dishes; let the syrup boil longer.

Quinces.—Pick out the finest quinces, pare them, and cut them in halves, or in rings; take the best of the parings and the seed, and boil them in water till they are very soft; strain the liquor, and have the kettle cleaned again; wash and weigh the quinces, and give them their weight in sugar; put the sugar in the water the parings were boiled in; skim it, and put in the quinces; let them boil very slowly till clear; take them up on dishes, and boil the syrup longer.

Citron Melon.—Cut it in pieces the size you wish, take out the soft centre and seeds, pare off the green rind, then throw the pieces in cold water and let them stand all night. Next day boil them, in water enough to cover them, for 20 minutes, adding alum the size of a walnut to each quart of water, to green them; ¾ sugar to 1 lb. fruit, slice some lemons, and put in also essence of ginger to taste. Boil till clear.—A. P.

Limes.—Green limes are found in our stores but for about 6 weeks in the middle of summer. Purchase them by the 100; put them in salt and water strong enough to bear an egg, (closely covered,) till the warm weather is over. Make an incision, take out all the seeds, and put them in cold water 24 hours, changing the water several times: then boil them in soda water till tender enough to put a straw through—say 1 tea-spoonful soda to 6 quarts water. Put them again in cold water for 24 hours, changing the water several times. To each pound limes 2½ lbs. white sugar, and 3 pints water. Boil the syrup 15 minutes, then put in the limes; boil them 5 minutes. They are then clear. Let syrup boil ¼ hour, and they are all done—100 limes make about 2 lbs. weight. These are delicious, and will keep always.

Peaches without Cooking.—To 4 lbs. fruit add 1 lb. sugar; place the sugar and peaches in a kettle over the fire, long enough to melt the sugar without cooking the fruit. Then remove them from the kettle, place them in Arthur's jars, and put them in a pot, (of warm water, if glass; hot, if tin,) letting the water boil several minutes.—M. L. N.

Damsons.—Weigh out as much sugar as you have fruit; if it is brown you must clarify it; put a pint of water to 3 lbs. of sugar, make a syrup, wash the damsons, put them in and let them cook slowly for ½ an hour; then take them out on dishes, and let them dry in the sun for 2 days, taking them in the house at night; boil the syrup ½ an hour after the fruit is taken out; when done in this way they will be whole and clear. You can make a jam by boiling them slowly for 2 hours; or a jelly, as currants.

Quince Marmalade.—Pare the quinces and cut them up fine; put the parings and cores to boil; then strain them; put in the quinces, and let them boil till soft; when mash them fine, and put in $\tfrac{3}{4}$ lb. of sugar to a lb. fruit; let them cook gently for 2 hours, and take them up in pint bowls; when cold, put brandy papers on the top of each, and paste them over; they will turn out whole to put on table.

Marmalade of Mixed Fruits.—Pare equal quantities of peaches, apples, pears and quinces; cut them fine, and put them to boil with a pint of water to 6 lbs. of fruit; let them cook thoroughly, but do not let them burn; take them out and mash them well; clean the kettle, and put them back, with half their weight in sugar; let them cook very slowly for 2 hours.

To Conserve Peaches.—Take the yellow peaches, pare them, and cut them from the stone in one piece; to 6 lbs. of peaches have 2 lbs. of sugar; make a syrup of $\tfrac{3}{4}$ lb. of sugar, and a little water; put them in, and let them stay till they are quite clear; then take them up carefully on a dish, and set them in the sun to dry; pound the sugar fine, and strew over them, turning them over to let each part have some; do not put much on at a time, and if any syrup is made remove them to fresh dishes; when they are sufficiently dry, lay them lightly in a jar, with a little sugar between each layer.

Frosted Fruit.—Take large ripe cherries, apricots, plums or grapes; if cherries, cut off half of the stem; have in one dish some white of an egg beaten, and in another some powdered loaf-sugar; take the fruit, one at a time, and roll them first in the egg, and then in the sugar; lay them on a sheet of white paper in a sieve, and set it on the top of a stove, or near a fire, till the icing is hard.

Crystalized Plums.—Stone them and put 1 lb. plums to ½ lb. sugar: cook them to a pulp: then spread on broad dishes to dry: pack them away in glass jars. When wanted to serve, take a little and roll in powdered sugar the shape of plums.—M. L. N.

Peach Leather.—Stew peaches as if for pies, taking out the stones and making into a pulp: put this on planed boards on a roof in the sun; in a few days it will be dry enough to peel off the boards. Roll it, and put away dry.

Cranberries.—For every quart cranberries put 1 lb. of white sugar: make a syrup first, skim it, and stew the cranberries; 1 dessert-spoonful of sup. car. soda put in after they are taken off the fire, takes off the acidity.

Cranberries are said to be nearly, or quite as good, if to 1 of stewed dried apples, 3 quarts of cranberries; or 1 of cranberries, and 2 apples.

Preserves keep with less cooking, if after being boiled awhile, they are taken out of their syrup and dried in the sun: the juice being put in glass jars, and standing also in the sun.—E. R. P.

Quinces and peaches are better and far less troublesome, preventing burning, by chipping them, and letting them boil till clear, doing the jelly longer and taking them out before going to pulp.

Pears.—Take sound medium-sized pears: remove nearly all the stem, and boil them in water just enough to cover them till soft; take each out carefully, and lay on a sieve to drain; put equal weight of sugar, the juice and rind of lemons; make a syrup of $\frac{1}{2}$ pint water to 1 lb. sugar, and boil them, (with green ginger, in a book-muslin bag,) till clear. If the syrup is not thickish, boil it longer.

Quinces, just as above, leaving out lemons and ginger.

Crab Apples.—Select perfect ones; pour boiling water over them, which removes the skin: lay them in water enough to cover them; let them simmer slowly till soft; take them out and drain; make a clean syrup, pound for pound; boil them in it till clear, lay them on dishes to cool, and place in jars; cook the syrup a little longer, and pour it over the apples when hot. Seal.

Peaches.—These may be done to taste even better than the hermetically sealed uncooked article, by taking half sugar, (or less,) to 1 lb. peaches. Cook them 5 minutes, the syrup somewhat longer. Seal them perfectly.

A Simpler Way.—Take the fruit, either quinces or peaches, which is not so nice, and cut off the whole peach or quince, in small pieces, sugar to taste; cook 20 minutes, and seal entirely from the air. Any kind of fruits we have in our markets may be thus preserved, at quarter the cost, time and trouble, and they will be found far better eating than preserves. *Method.*—Let the glass jars be warming near the fire, while the fruit is stewing; have corks to fit, bladder lined, put in the fruit a little at a time, boiling hot; warm your cement, meanwhile, insert the cork, taking care to have the glass full to the cork, press down tightly; then put another piece of wet bladder over the cork, tieing it down tightly; invert the glass into the cement, then stand it up to harden; when hard, roll the edge of the glass again in the hot cement, and you have a perfectly air-tight vessel. The very best and safest mode, however, and one which servants must be doubly-refined stupid not to succeed in, is HARTELL'S PATENT SELF-SEALING JARS. We give, below, an engraving of one of these valuable vessels.

Hartell's Self-Sealing Jar.

These vessels were used during the last summer in incredibly large quantities, and with the most complete success. They may be obtained in most of the principal cities and towns in the country, of the agents. They are accompanied with explicit directions for use, and valuable recipes for putting up fruits and vegetables.

We are glad to be able, from actual trial, to give this strong testimonial in favour of so useful an invention.

The following methods of Preserving Fruits, etc., have been practically tested, the two past seasons, with the *Hartell Jar*, and ,if carefully followed, will not only be found to succeed, but the whole operation of putting up Winter Stores will be found so easy and simple, that the most inexperienced housekeeper need never fail. *Fruit* and *Vegetables* put up *fresh* in these Jars, are admitted by medical men to be far more wholesome and nutritious than by the old plan of cooking—most of the leading physicians in this city having them in use. Metal Jars or Covers have long been considered objectionable for preserving anything containing acidity, and the Hartell Jar, being wholly of glass, and fastened and unfastened in a moment by a slight turn of the cover, and requiring no cement, will be found upon trial to be a *perfect success.*

One thing should be borne in mind, and that a very important one, in selecting *Fruit* for preserving, that which is fairly ripe, without softness or bruises should be preferred, and the same rule will apply to Vegetables. Tomatoes should be chosen with as much *flesh* and as little seed as possible. The Hartell Jar and Cover being wholly of glass, care should be taken *not* to put a *hot cover* on a cold Jar, or the reverse, as the difference in temperature may cause one or the other to break; but in heating up be careful to place the cover *loosely* on the Jar, so they may be of equal temperature when filled, and should you boil them in any vessel to expel the air, place a cloth or some straw on its bottom to prevent the glass from heating too suddenly at one point, by coming in contact with the bottom of the vessel

Peaches.—Pare the peaches; halve or quarter; then pack in the Jar as closely as possible. Put the cover on loosely and place in a cool oven, then raise the heat gradually until Jar and Fruit is heated through. Then take out of the oven and fill up the Jar to the top with boiling syrup, (say one-quarter or half a pound of sugar to a quart of water); then screw on the cover, tighten, and when cool invert the Jar to see that it is perfectly tight; should it leak, give another turn to the cover.

Peaches, No. 2.—After they are pared and halved, weigh them; then take quarter their weight of sugar, with sufficient water to dissolve it, put on to boil, and, if dark, clear with isinglass; if clear, skim it; put in the peaches, let them come to a boil; have ready and at hand the Jars well heated, and fill *entirely* to the brim; then screw on the covers, and when nearly cool ascertain by trying with the hand whether the covers are perfectly tight.

Pears may be prepared in the same way, less sugar being required for fruits with less acid.

Tomatoes.—*Whole.*—Choose thick flesh and little seed; skin them; squeeze out seeds as dry as possible; place the pulp in the Jars; put on the cover; set the Jar in cold water, bring to boiling point; boil five minutes, then tighten cover.

Second plan.—After skinning, season to taste, and cook ready for the table; place in a heated Jar while hot, and tighten cover.

Tomatoes may be kept perfectly by being cooked twenty minutes, and screwing them up while boiling hot in the Jars, also well heated.

Quinces.—Pare, and halve or quarter; put

them in water and boil until tender, then place the fruit in the Jar hot; put a quarter pound of sugar to the quart of water that the Quinces have been boiled in; boil the syrup, and pour on the fruit until the Jar is full, while it is boiling; tighten and set away.

PLUMS can be preserved very fine by following directions for Peaches No. 1, and instead of peeling prick the skin with a pin.

CHERRIES, seeded, and such fruits as STRAWBERRIES, BLACKBERRIES, RASPBERRIES, etc., may be sprinkled with sugar, and allowed to stand a short time until the juice begins to start; then place them in the preserving kettle; just allow them to come to a boil, then place in Jars as other fruit.

The above Recipes have been tried by a great many persons with entire success, but we are free to admit that the business of putting up Fresh Fruits is yet only in its infancy, and we have heard of several persons the past season putting up Peaches, etc., in the Hartell Jar, without syrup—using water alone.

Hartell & Letchworth, No. 13 North Fifth St., Philadelphia, are the sole manufacturers under the Patent, and they will take pleasure in showing these Jars to all who are interested.

Raspberry Jam.—1 quart raspberries, 1 pint currant jelly bruised well together; set them over a slow fire, stirring till it boils; after boiling 5 minutes, cool, and pour into glasses, as currant jelly, or into moulds.

SYRUPS.

Strawberry Syrup.—Juice 1 pint, water do., white sugar 3 lbs. After squeezing the juice from berries, take the pulp and pour the measured water over it, and let it come to a boil; strain this, and make up the pint with water, if wanting. Pour this on the sugar, put it over the fire, and heat till the sugar is dissolved and come to a boil; take it off the fire, add strawberry juice, stir well; place on the fire 5 minutes, remove, and when cool strain and bottle. Same for Raspberry, Pine Apple, &c. : 3 quarts ripe berries make the above.

Vanilla Syrup.—Boil 3 lbs. white sugar in 1 quart boiling water, ¼ hour; then put in 2 Vanilla beans and 1 tea-cup water, and boil until reduced to 1 quart again. Then strain it through a flannel bag and bottle close.

Lemon Syrup.—Squeeze the juice of 25 lemons : strain it, and add 1 pint water, 2 lbs. sugar. Let it simmer. Bottle it.

Ginger Syrup.—1 lb. sugar to 1 pint water: boil 20 minutes—when cool, add essence of ginger to taste.

Cherry Vinegar.—6 quarts cherries, broken up, and 1 quart vinegar ; let it stand 3 days : then press the juice from them through a jelly bag, and to 1 pint juice ¾ lb. white sugar : boil it 12 minutes, and skim. This makes 8 porter bottles full. Blackberries done in this way are also good as a drink.—A. R.

PLEASANT DRINKS.

Lemonade.—To 1 pint juice 4 lbs. sugar, 2 quarts ice-water. It makes more to soak the halves of lemons that have been squeezed in a little water, a few at a time, using the water.

Mock Lemonade.—$\frac{1}{4}$ oz. tartaric acid, 6 oz. sugar, 4 drops essence lemon dropped on the sugar, 1 quart boiling water.

Carbonated Drink.—2 quarts ice-water, 4 table-spoonfuls vinegar, 2 tea-spoonfuls ground ginger. Sweeten to taste, and add 1 tea-spoonful soda, 1 do. cream tartar.

Penny Beer.—$\frac{3}{4}$ oz. cream tartar, 1 cts. worth sassafras, 1 do. sarsaparilla, 1 do. pipsissaway. All these are bought in the market. Put 1 gallon water to the sassafras, pipsissaway and sarsaparilla, and boil 1½ hours Then pour it off and add another gallon of water, and boil until the strength is out of the herbs Pour it boiling on the cream tartar: when about milk warm put in 1 cts. worth yeast. Sweeten with molasses and sugar.

Raspberry Vinegar.—Pour 1 quart vinegar on 1 quart fresh-picked raspberries: the next day strain it through a sieve on another quart of raspberries, and so on 5 or 6 days; then to every pint juice add 1 lb. white sugar, set it in a jar, which must be placed in a pot of boiling water, until scalded through. Bottle.

Ginger Beer.—1 gallon cold water, 1 lb. white sugar, ½ oz. race ginger, 1 sliced lemon, 1 tea-cup yeast. Let it stand all night to ferment; then pour it off without stirring, bottle it, and add 1 raisin to each bottle.—M. M.

Hoarhound Beer.—Take 1 handful flour, pour 1 quart boiling water over it, 4 table-spoonfuls of yeast, and put in when cool enough; when risen, add 3 lbs. brown sugar, 4 table-spoonfuls ground ginger, 1 pint strong hoarhound, (4 cents' worth,) steep it in boiling water: stir this all up, let it be for 12 hours, strain through a linen cloth into bottles.

Portable Lemonade.—Tartaric acid ½ oz., loaf sugar 3 ounces, essence of lemon ½ drachm. Powder the tartaric acid : also the sugar. Mix them, and pour the essence of lemon upon them a few drops at a time; when all is mixed, divide into 12 equal parts, and put them in white paper. When wanted, dissolve 1 in a tumbler of water, and lemonade will be the result.

Currant Wine.—To 1 quart juice add 2 quarts water, 1 lb. sugar; mix well together, and let it stand 24 hours, without stirring : then skim it, putting it in a jug or keg, leaving out the cork, and let it ferment in a cool place for a week, or till done fermenting : then cork tightly, and when clear it is fit to bottle.

Quince Wine.—Grate whole quinces, (cutting out rot and worms,) squeeze the juice through a flannel bag, and to each quart juice put 1 lb. sugar. Let it work long enough to clear out the pugs : when clear bottle it.—M. P.

A Pleasant Wine—2 quarts morel cherry juice, 1 quart water, and 2 lbs. sugar : boil and skim it, and when cool add 1 pint brandy.

GAS COOKING.

In regard to cooking with gas, our experience is just 3 months old. As far as that experience goes, we give it a decided preference over every other kind of cooking.

The best apparatus for the purpose is Gleason's Patent, to be had of Gleason & Sons, No. 1227 Market street. There are two sizes; one of them small enough for the smallest family—very compact and convenient, and not unsightly—they cost from 20 to 30 dollars.

The usual objection made to the use of gas for cooking, has been, that it is expensive. We have not found it so—and for labour-saving and cleanliness, nothing can equal it.

Bread baked by gas is not to be surpassed for its delicate taste; and meats retain their flavour and tenderness more perfectly than when roasted by any other means—for steaks and chops it equals "the good hickory coals," of which this generation is often reminded by the one which is passing away; and when it is remembered that the heat is only generated while the stove is in actual use, its superiority over every other mode of cooking is obvious for the summer months.

One of our friends, who has used gas for this purpose for 15 years, both summer and winter, and who is acquainted with the methods pursued in Paris and London, assures us that it is as much cheaper than either coal or wood, as it is better. If that is so, there is really nothing to be desired but some improvement in the apparatus, which could be easily made to make cooking a pleasure, instead of a temper-trying burden.—E. W. T.

COOKERY FOR THE SICK.

LET every thing be sweet and clean, as their senses of taste and smell are very acute. Let it be presented in an inviting form; fine China, silver, &c., used. Be careful not to over-flavour their food. Always have a shawl at hand; also, a clean towel, clean handkerchief, and a small waiter, when you present food or drink. Many of the articles under "dessert" are good for the sick. It is well to have a stand or small table by the bedside, that you can set any thing on. A small silver strainer that will just fit over a tumbler or tea-cup, is very useful to strain lemonade, panada, or herb tea. If you want any thing to use through the night, you should prepare it, if possible, beforehand; as a person that is sick, can sometimes fall asleep without knowing it, if the room is kept perfectly still.

A Vegetable Soup.—Take an onion, a turnip, 2 pared potatoes, a carrot (a head of celery, or not): boil them in 3 pints water till the vegetables are cooked; add a little salt; have a slice of bread toasted and buttered, put into a bowl and pour soup over. When in season, tomatoes, or okra, or both, improve this.

Gum Water.—$\frac{1}{2}$ oz. to 1 oz. dissolved in 1 quart cold water. Sweeten it.

Slippery Elm Bark.—Very good for weak or inflamed eyes.

Coffee.—Sick persons should have their coffee

made separate from the family, as standing in the tin pot spoils the flavour. Put 2 tea-spoonfuls of ground coffee in a small mug, and pour boiling water on it; let it set by the fire to settle, and pour it off in a cup, with sugar and cream. Care should be taken that there are no burnt grains.

Chocolate.—To make a cup of chocolate, grate a large tea-spoonful in a mug, and pour a tea-cup of boiling water on it; let it stand covered by the fire a few minutes, when you can put in sugar and cream.

Black Tea.—Black tea is much more suitable than green for sick persons, as it does not affect the nerves. Put a tea-spoonful in a pot that will hold about 2 cups, and pour boiling water on it. Let it set by the fire to draw 5 or 10 minutes.

Rye Mush.—This is a nourishing and light diet for the sick, and is by some preferred to mush made of Indian meal. Four large spoonfuls of rye flour mixed smooth in a little water, and stirred in a pint of boiling water: let it boil 20 minutes, stirring frequently. Nervous persons who sleep badly, rest much better after a supper of corn, or rye mush, than if they take tea or coffee.

Boiled Custard.—Beat an egg with a heaped tea-spoonful of sugar; stir it into a tea-cupful of boiled milk, and stir till it is thick; pour it in a bowl on a slice of toast cut up, and grate a little nutmeg over.

Panada.—Put some crackers, crusts of dry bread or dried rusk, in a sauce-pan with cold water, and a few raisins; after it has boiled half an hour, put in sugar, nutmeg, and ½ a glass of wine, if the patient has no fever. If you have dried rusk, it is a quicker way to put the rusk in a bowl with some sugar, and pour boiling water on it out of the tea-kettle. If the patient can take nothing but liquids, this makes a good drink when strained.

Egg Panada.—Boil a handful of good raisins in a quart of water; toast a slice of bread and cut it up; beat 2 eggs with a spoonful of sugar, and mix it with the bread; when the raisins are done, pour them on the toast and eggs, stirring all the time; season to your taste with wine, nutmeg and butter.

Barley Panada.—Boil a small tea-cup of barley in water till it is soft, with a tea-cup of raisins; put in nutmeg and sugar, and break in it toast or dried rusk.

Calf's Foot Blancmange.—Put a set of nicely-cleaned feet in 4 quarts of water, and let it boil more than half away; strain through a colander, and when it is cold scrape off all the fat, and take out that which settles at the bottom; put it in a sauce-pan, with a quart of new milk, sugar to your taste, lemon peal and juice, and cinnamon or mace; let it boil 10 minutes and strain it; wet your moulds, and when it is nearly cold, put it in them; when it is cold and stiff, it can be turned out on a plate, and eaten with or without cream. This is very nice for a sick person, and is easily made.

Chicken Water.—If you have a small chicken, it will take half of it to make a pint of chicken water. Cut it up and put it to boil in a covered skillet with a quart of water; when it has boiled down to a pint, take it up, and put in a little salt and slice of toasted bread. This is valuable in cases of dysentery and cholera morbus, particularly when made of old fowls.

Beef Tea, &c.—Take a piece of juicy beef, without any fat, cut it in small pieces, bruise it till tender, put it in a wide-mouthed bottle, and cork it tight; put this in a pot of cold water, set it over the fire, and let it boil an hour or more. When a person can take but a small quantity of nourishment, this is very good. Mutton may be done in the same way.

Mutton and Veal Broth.—Boil a piece of mutton till it comes to pieces; then strain the broth, and let it get cold, so that the fat will rise, which must be taken off; then warm it, and put in a little salt. Veal broth may be made in the same way, and is more delicate for sick persons.

Wine Whey.—Boil a pint of milk, and put to it a glass of white wine; set it over the fire till it just boils again, then set it off till the curd has settled, when strain it, and sweeten to your taste.

Oat-meal Gruel.—Mix 2 spoonfuls of oatmeal with as much water as will mix it easily, and stir it in a pint of boiling water in a sauce-pan until perfectly smooth; let it boil a few minutes; season it with sugar and nutmeg, and pour it out on a slice of bread toasted and cut up, or some dried rusk. If the patient should like them, you can put in a few raisins, stoned and cut up. This will keep good a day, and if nicely warmed over, is as good as when fresh.

Corn Gruel.—Mix 2 spoonfuls of sifted cornmeal in some water; have a clean skillet with a pint of boiling water in it, stir it in, and when done, season it with salt to your taste, or sugar, if you prefer it.

Arrow-Root.—Moisten 2 tea-spoonfuls of powdered arrow-root with water, and rub it smooth with a spoon; then pour on a half pint of boiling water; season it with lemon juice, or wine and nutmeg. In cooking arrow-root for children, it is a very good way to make it very thick, and thin it afterwards with milk.

Blackberries.—Allow a pint of currant juice and a pint of water to 6 lbs. of blackberries; give them their weight in brown sugar; let them boil till they appear to be done, and the syrup is rich. Blackberry jelly can be made as currant jelly, and is good for sick children, mixed with water.

Blackberry Syrup.—The following is the recipe for making the famous blackberry syrup. No family should be without it. All who try it will find it a sovereign remedy for bowel complaints :—"To 2 quarts blackberry juice add $\frac{1}{2}$ oz. each of powdered nutmeg, cinnamon and allspice, and $\frac{1}{4}$ oz. powdered cloves. Boil these together to get the strength of the spices, and to preserve the berry juice. While hot, add a pint of fourth proof pure French brandy, and sweeten with loaf sugar. Give a child 2 tea-spoonfuls 3 times a day, and if the disorder is not checked, add to the quantity."

Barley Water.—Take 2 oz. of pearl barley, wash it in clean cold water, put it into $\frac{1}{2}$ pint boiling water, and let it boil for 5 minutes: pour off this water, and add to it 2 quarts of boiling water; boil it to 2 pints, and strain; flavour it with lemon juice; sweeten with white sugar to your taste.

For Chapped Lips.—Put a tea-cupful of rich cream over some coals to stew, with 3 tablespoonfuls of powdered loaf-sugar. This has a healing effect.

Another remedy, equally good, is to a tea-cupful of honey, add half the quantity of mutton tallow, and stew together till well mixed; pour it out in a cup, and keep stirring till cold.

For chapped hands, mix together equal quantities of rich cream and strong vinegar, and rub it over every time you wash your hands.

Cold Water for Burns.—Mr. Seth Hunt, of Northampton, gives the following statement of the success of treating with cold water a severe burn and scald in his family:—" Cold water was applied, by immersion, till the pain ceased; the water being changed as often as it became warm. The part was then kept swathed with wet bandages, a dry woolen one enveloping them, until the injury was healed. The healing was rapid, and effected without leaving a scar. The instant relief which the cold water gave from the excruciating pain, was highly gratifying."

Liebig's Broth for the Sick.—For one portion of broth take ½ lb. freshly killed meat (beef or chicken), cut it into small pieces, and add to it 1⅛ lbs. pure water to which have been added 4 drops muriatic acid, and ½ to 1 drachm of salt: mix them well together. After standing an hour the whole is strained through a hair sieve, allowing it to pass through without pressing or squeezing. The portion passing through first being cloudy it is again poured through the sieve, and this process is repeated until it becomes perfectly clear. Upon the residue of meat remaining in the sieve, $\frac{1}{2}$ lb. pure water is poured, in small portions. In this manner, about 1 lb. of liquid (cold extract of meat) is obtained, of a red colour and pleasant meat-broth taste. It is administered to the sick, cold, by the cupfull, according to their inclination. It must not be heated, as it becomes cloudy thereby, and a thick coagulum is deposited. A great hindrance to the employment of this broth is, in summer, its liability to change in warm weather: it commences regularly to ferment, like sugar water with yeast, without the usual odour. On account of this, the meat must be extracted with perfectly cold water, and in a cool place. Ice water and refrigeration with ice, completely removes this difficulty. Most important of all is it, that the meat should be perfectly fresh. This broth is now in use in the hospitals, and in the private practice of several of the most distinguished physicians of Munich. "This preparation," says Liebig, "was first induced by a case of typhus fever occuring in my family; that, in a certain stage of this disease, the greatest difficulty met with by the physician lay in incomplete digestion, a consequence of the condition of the intestines; and besides, in the want of nutriment proper for digestion and the formation of blood. The common broths prepared for the sick are deficient here. This new broth contains, besides meat albumen, a certain quantity of hematin and therein a far greater quantity of iron, necessary for the formation of the blood corpuscles, and finally the digesting chloihydic acid."

Racahout.—*Food for Invalids.*—Rice flour 5 oz.; arrow-root 5 oz.; powdered sugar 8 oz.; cocoa 2 oz.; vanilla bean 2 drachms. Rub the sugar and vanilla together, and then mix *all* together. A good substitute may be prepared by mixing together 1 tea-spoonful of vanilla chocolate, a level table-spoonful of arrow-root, do. of rice flour; this will make 1 pint.

To prepare racahout for the sick, take 1 or 2 table-spoonfuls of the mixture (according as it be desired thick or thin), rub it up with a little cold milk, and stir into a pint of boiling milk; boil 15 minutes, and sweeten to taste.

WINTER AND OTHER STORES.

VEGETABLES are best kept on a stone floor, if the air be excluded. Meat in a cold, dry place. Sugar and sweetmeats require a dry place—so does salt. Candles cold, but not damp. Dried meats, hams, &c., the same. All sorts of seeds for puddings, soups, &c., are best in glass jars, with close lids. I prefer glass for every household purpose for which it is at all suitable, its contents being seen at a glance. It is quite cheap, if bought in quantity. Whitalls, Race st., near Fourth, keep jars and bottles.

Corn.—There are several methods. Cutting off the cob after cooking 5 minutes, is one—then drying in the sun. Another is to make a pickle instead of drying it, and put in "Arthur's Cans." The Shakers have the art.

Another Way to keep Green Corn.—Make pickle in a barrel, as for meat. Throw into it, from time to time, ears of unhusked sugar corn. When you have enough, put weights to keep the corn under, and cover the barrel. When used, soak the ears all night, (after taking off the husk,) and boil in a large portion of water, which must be changed once, in boiling.

Okra.—This very desirable vegetable for soups, should be purchased when young and small, sliced, and dried on plates, in a cool oven, or about a stove. Put it away in glass jars, dry.

Herbs should be gathered when they are in blossom.

There are various ways of keeping eggs: all those given below are good.

Greased Eggs.—Warm some fat of almost any kind, put the eggs in; cover them quite, take them out and lay them in an old tin or earthen vessel: paste them up, or better, cement with the tin, as named elsewhere, and they will be found good all winter. Some use gum water.

Eggs in Lime.—Pour 2 gallons hot water over 1 pint lime, and ½ pint salt; when cold put some eggs in a jar, and pour it over them; be sure there are no cracked ones.—R. H.

Keeping Eggs.—Having tried many ways of preserving eggs, I have found the following to be the easiest, cheapest, surest, and best. Take your crock, keg, or barrel, according to the quantity you have, cover the bottom with half an inch salt, and set your eggs close together on the small end; be very particular to put the small end down; for if put in any other position, they will not keep as well, and the yelk will adhere to the shell: sprinkle them over with salt, so as to fill the interstices, and then put in another layer of eggs, and cover with salt, and so on, till your vessel is filled. Cover it tight, and put it where it will not freeze, and the eggs will keep perfectly fresh and good any desirable length of time.

Sweet Potatoes.—These are the greatest luxury in the way of vegetables, our tables can offer in winter. Engage a Jerseyman, in whom you have confidence, to bring them at the proper time in a proper state. Let them be put in the garret of a house which has a furnace, in barrels or boxes: let them be uncovered for several days, with a circulation of air constantly kept up. At the end of 4 or 5 days cover them with newspapers, if the boxes have no covers. I find the temperature most adapted to them is 60. We have them till they come again.—E. N.

White Potatoes are hardy, and will bear the cellar.

Lima Beans, picked ripe, and put on a garret floor to dry; then shelled and put in bags in a dry place, will keep. Soak them over night.

To keep Apples and Pears.—Put them in air-tight vessels, and place them in the cellar in a temperature between 32 and 40. In this way, says the "Horticulturist," these fruits may be preserved, in perfect order for eating, all winter.

Another Way.—Wrapping each apple or pear in paper, answers well also.

Peaches Uncooked.—Procure glass jars, (with a rim at the top, and not too thick bottoms.) Pare and halve ripe peaches, put them into the jars, (which must be warmed previously,) packing as close as possible in the jars. Make a syrup of 1 lb. sugar to 1 quart water; let it come to a boil, then pour it over the peaches, filling the jars quite full. Have ready some white muslin, and ¼ yard gum elastic cloth. Dip the muslin, which may be cut in squares of one-eighth yard size, into the syrup: then have the gum cloth ready cut, and tie the two together with strong twine tightly over the bottle. This was tried with entire success, the concave lids proving the absent air. I should think tomatoes would do well thus, if cooked, especially. This gum cloth may be had at gum elastic stores, at $1 25 per yard, and it will last years, with care.—S. L.

To Keep Eggs.—During a long voyage to South America, it was noticed how fresh the eggs continued to be. The steward was called on for his secret. He said that as he purchased his stock, he packed it down in small boxes—raisin boxes—and afterwards, about once a week, turned over every box but the one out of which he was using. This was all. The reason of his success is, that by turning the eggs over, he kept the yolks about the middle of the albumen. If still, the yolk will after a while find its way through the white to the shell, and when it does so, the egg will spoil. Hens understand this fact, for they, as is well known, turn over their eggs on which they set, at least daily.

To Tell Good Eggs.—If you desire to be certain that your eggs are good and fresh, put them in water. If the buts turn up they are not fresh. This is an infallible rule to distinguish a good egg from a bad one.

Tomatoes, &c.—Cook and season them as for dinner, omitting sugar, bread, or flour. Put them boiling hot, either into "Hartell's Jars," or have glass bottles with fitting corks ready (warming the glass), and fill them with the hot tomato. Place a piece of bladder under the cork before you insert it: put it in tightly; now insert the glass quickly into a cup of cement: let it cool, and dip again.

MISCELLANEOUS.

German Puffs.—1 pint milk; 2 eggs beaten together; add milk and flour gradually to the eggs; a little salt. Grease 4 tea-cups with butter, and put the beaten batter in, about $\frac{2}{3}$ full.

Trifle.—Take slices of sponge cake and place them in the bottom of a glass dish: on this put thin slices of citron, or preserved apple: pour over this a boiled custard, and on the top put a whip. (*See p.* 67.)

Preserved Orange Skins.—Cut them into strips the size of a straw, and boil them in a syrup till clear. Keep them to use for Bird's Nest pudding.

Apple Tapioca.—Pare, core, and quarter 8 apples; take $\frac{1}{2}$ table-spoonful tapioca which has been soaked all night in water. Put in $\frac{1}{2}$ tea-cup of white sugar, and flavour. Put this tapioca, so mixed, in a stewpan, and let it simmer 10 minutes. Then put in the apples and simmer 10 minutes more. When cold, there will be a jelly round the apples.

Orange Cocoa Nut.—Break up a fine ripe cocoa nut. Peel off the brown skin and wash the slices in cold water. Then grate it into a pan and sweeten it with powdered white sugar. Have ready some fine large ripe oranges. First peel them, and then cut them into round slices rather thick, and remove all the seeds carefully. Cover with slices of orange the bottom of a large glass bowl, making them very sweet with fine sugar; then put a thick layer of grated cocoa nut; then a layer of orange slices; then more cocoa nut, and so on, till the bowl is well filled, finishing with cocoa nut heaped high on the top.

Iced Grapes.—Take large, close bunches of fine, ripe, thin-skinned grapes, and remove any that are imperfect. Tie a string in a loop to the top of the stem. Strain into a deep dish a sufficient quantity of white of egg. Dip the bunches of grapes into it, immersing them thoroughly. Then drain them, and roll them about in a flat dish of finely-powdered loaf sugar till they are completely coated with it, using your fingers to spread the sugar into the hollows between the grapes. Hang up the bunches by the strings, till the icing is entirely dry. They should be dried in a warm place.

Ripe currants may be iced as above. Raspberries, strawberries, ripe gooseberries, plums, and cherries may be thus dipped in white of egg, and rolled in sugar.

Ice Cream.—Take 2 quarts good country cream; sweeten it with 1 lb. white sugar. Take $\frac{1}{2}$ a vanilla bean and grate it on a nutmeg grater into a little of the cream: scald this to extract the flavour: boil 1 table-spoonful arrow-root in $\frac{1}{2}$ pint *milk:* mix all together: put it into the freezer, stir it frequently, scraping the frozen parts from the sides often: *beat it* from time to time, while freezing: the more it is beaten, the lighter and more of it.

Tomato Figs.—Scald and remove the skins from 8 lbs. tomatoes: cook them in 3 lbs. sugar till clear: take them out with a perforated spoon, on dishes; dry them in the sun or a cool oven, turning them occasionally. When dry, pack them in a box, sprinkling sugar between the layers. Round, middle size tomatoes are the best.

To Preserve Sour Plums.—Pour boiling hot water over them, let them come to a boil: pour off this water and make a syrup of 4 lbs. sugar to 6 lbs. plums; cook till done, and put up hot in Arthur's jars.

Preserved Tomatoes.—To each lb. of large tomatoes 1 lb. brown sugar, and 1 large lemon. Grate the peel into one vessel and squeeze the juice into another: scald and peel the tomatoes and put them in a kettle with the sugar and grated peel; boil them slowly $1\frac{1}{2}$ hours: skim well: then add juice and boil $\frac{1}{2}$ hour longer: when done, pour into stone jars, *hot*.

Preserved Apples.—Pare and core some R. I. Greenings: wash and weigh them: to each lb. apples put $\frac{3}{4}$ lb. sugar. Make a syrup; let it boil awhile and skim: place the fruit carefully in; watch that it does not boil too hard: remove them, when tender, on plates, to cool and toughen: have 2 lemons cut into very thin slices (seeds out), and boil 5 minutes in jelly. When all is cold, pour syrup over apples.

Potato Biscuit.—$1\frac{1}{4}$ lbs. flour, 8 medium size potatoes, 3 oz. butter or lard, $\frac{1}{2}$ tea-cupful good home-made yeast, (if lard, a tea-spoonful salt). Let them get very light, then make them out, and let them get very light again. Bake in a quick oven.

Sour Milk Bread.—When bread or cakes

are made of sour milk or cream, as a general rule, 1 tea-spoonful of sub. car. soda is sufficient for 1 pint of milk; *no cream of tartar.* *Soft dough, and a quick oven*, are essential to the production of light cakes, &c.

Quick Milk Biscuit.—2 lbs. flour, ¼ lb. lard, small bowl milk, 2 medium size potatoes, 1 tea-cup yeast, *all warm.* Raise in a warm place, cut them out, let them get very light. Bake in a very hot oven.

Another.—1 pint of bread sponge, 2 potatoes, mashed fine; butter, the size of a walnut; 1 egg added last. Stir, and put to rise.—M. W.

Sweet Potato Rolls.—Boil 3 large sweet potatoes; while hot, make smooth and beat in ¼ lb. lard and 1 tea-spoonful of salt. Make a sponge of 2½ lbs. of flour, and stir in the potatoes; 1 tea-cup of yeast; let it stand 8 hours; make into little rolls; avoid all kneading and handling; let them rise again, and bake in a quick oven.—M. D.

Light Gingerbread.—Take 3 cups of molasses, 5 of flour, 1 of sugar, 3 eggs, 1 tea-spoonful of soda, 2 of cream tartar; (dissolve these, apart, in rose water,) work the sugar with ¼ lb. butter, put 1 table-spoonful of cloves, and do. of ginger. Mix and bake in cups or shallow pans.

Hamlin Cake.—1 cup of flour; 1 do. of sugar; 3 eggs; the rind grated and juice of 1 lemon; 1 tea-spoonful of soda and 2 cream tar. mixed together; use 1 spoonful of the mixture only. Drop this batter in small quantities, apart, and sprinkle with chopped pea-nuts or shell barks or walnuts.

HINTS FOR WASHING AND IRONING DAYS.

CONCENTRATED LYE, OR SAPONIFIER.

Hard Soap.—To 1 lb. of the Saponifier add 3 gallons of water, dissolve in an iron or copper kettle, heat to boiling : add 5 lbs. of tallow, soap-fat, lard or olive oil, until a clear solution of uniform consistency is obtained; when the solution has attained this point, keep on a simmer, and add 1 tea-cup full of salt, then the soap, separating first into hard grains, ceases to froth, and forms slabs and flakes through which the steam puffs, when it is finished and ready to mould. If you want to make rosin or yellow soap, take one-third of clean rosin and two-thirds of the above quantity of fat : add the rosin first, and when it is all dissolved and taken up by the Saponifier, put in the fat and finish up as the other.

Hard Fancy Soap.—Dissolve 1 lb. of Saponifier in 3 lbs. of water, and add thereto, stirring the same rapidly, 4 lbs. of tallow or soap-fat, merely liquefied—or that much lard or olive oil, cold ; keep stirring and beating until all has assumed the appearance of thick honey, cover it up and set the batch in a warm place, or better, cover it with a woolen blanket or a feather bed, to keep up the heat, and let it stand for 24 hours, when it will have set into a fine, hard soap, which may be perfumed and variegated with colours by stirring the desired colours or perfume into the mixture, just before covering.

Soft Soap.—To 1 lb. of the Saponifier add 3 gallons of rain or soft water : set it boiling, and then put in 4 lbs. of soap-fat or tallow. When the solution is clear and the fat all combined, which is seen by the disappearance of all fatty eyes or spots on the liquid, add 12 gallons of soft or rain water; when cold, your soap is ready for use.

For all other purposes in which potash is used, the Saponifier will prove a cheap substitute.

Pump water softened and made fit for washing : —dissolve 1 lb. of the Saponifier in 1 gallon of water, and keep it for use in a well-corked demijohn or jug; to a tub full of pump or hard spring water add from one-eighth of a gill to a pint of the clear solution ; the quantity of course varies according to the size of the tub and nature of the water, some taking more and some less ; a tablespoonful will generally be found enough to make 3 to 5 gallons of water fit for washing.

In all the above operations it should be remembered to replenish the water, which may evaporate while dissolving the Saponifier, or while boiling. The soft soap, made as above, I know to be excellent. The saponifier can be had at any of the drug stores.

Soap for Washing Clothes, &c.—*Ammonia Soap.*—Ammonia is a wonderfully cleansing principle, and I am inclined to believe, enters largely into all soaps vended, as " warranted to take out soil and grease in silk cloth," &c. Purchase 5 lbs. strong country soap, or else the home-made soap named on preceding page, cut it into thin pieces and put it into 1 quart strong lye : let it get hot enough to melt, not boil; when dissolved take it off the fire, and add ¼ oz. pearl ash, and 1 gill liquid ammonia. Have a crock or stone pot with a lid, into which pour the hot liquid before ammonia is put in. Cover it quickly, and stir 2 or 3 times while cooling, keeping it covered the while. When about to use it, take 1 lb. of it and dissolve in a basin of warm (not hot) water, meanwhile putting water for washing hot enough to bear your hands; put all together, stirring with hand, and put in as many clothes as the water will cover. Cover over the tub with a soiled sheet, and let it stand 20 minutes. When you wash the articles you will find the soil not removed, but loose, and very little rubbing needful. The washboard need not be used for the "first boil." Let all the clothes go through this tub, adding a little hot water, and they will be found surprisingly clean and white. Nearly all colours in calico and mousselines will bear it, but 'tis better to try a piece of it first. A little beef's gall put in, sets colours. When every article has gone through it, do not pour it under the gate, but set it aside till evening: water grape vines, and vegetables, and flowers with it, and a better fertilizer is not. Also, you may make a very useful soap of sand, by taking a pint of the soap while cooling, and mixing enough pewter sand to adhere. Make it in cakes and put to dry. This is good for scrubbing grease spots, &c., and invaluable on the wash-stand to take ink-spots from hands.

Tinware, passed through such suds, is cleansed and polished by the process, and washbasins, &c., may be rinsed after, and look well.

Flannels are best put into the suds when it is nearly or quite cold: it prevents their fulling, somewhat. Boiling suds must be improper for woolen goods, as fullers use that method to thicken their woolen fabrics.

The great cause of flannel shrinking is, I believe, the oil and perspiration from the pores of the body; therefore an article half cotton is preferable.

To make Calicoes Wash Well.—Infuse 3 gills of salt in 4 quarts of boiling water, and put the calicoes in while hot, and leave it till cold; in this way the colours are rendered permanent, and will not fade by subsequent washing.

Bleaching Muslin.—Chemists allow $\frac{1}{2}$ lb. chloride of lime, dissolved in 1 gal. boiling water. Care must be taken in using it, because, if very strong, the fabric will be tendered: not otherwise. It will be better to consult a chemist, however, before putting any muslin goods into the solution. The chloride of lime used in chemistry being of such different degrees of strength, the fabric may be made tender, and ruined for use.

The Patent Clothes-Drying Machine.—This is the most simple and useful machine ever yet invented for drying clothes. It is simply a post erected in the centre of the yard, about $6\frac{1}{2}$ feet above the surface, or of a proper height to be out of the way of the head. In the centre of the upper end of the post is driven an iron pin, projecting about 3 inches. A cast-iron hub, having a hole in the centre of the lower arch of the size of the pin, with 6 mortices or recesses at equal distances around the periphery; the hub is placed upon the pin in the post, the arms, 6 in number, are placed one in each mortice or recess. The clothes line is run from arm to arm around the machine from 6 to 8 times, and about 8 inches apart. The washerwoman stands on a chair, having her basket of clothes by her side, and hangs the small ones first on the inner line, moving the machine around until she has hung out her entire washing without moving her chair. Every little breath of air causes it to revolve around; thus the clothes are constantly changing position—allowing the sun and air to come to all of them alike. The advantages are—

1. That when there are no clothes on the machine, it is out of the way of the head, and can all be unshipped and put away, leaving nothing but the post in the yard.

2. It will dry the clothes in a much less time.

3. There is no necessity for treading down the plants in the yard, as only one position is necessary.

4. Clothes can be hung out in much less time.

5. A person can pass around the machine to any other part of the yard without stooping under the clothes, as is the case when the line is strung across the yard.

6. Their cheapness, as one can be furnished, complete and erected, for $5 00—if turned post and painted, $6 00. To be had at 1020 Chestnut street.

Starch.—It is economy to use two kinds of clear starch in a wash. The Pearl starch is best for shirts and collars, &c. Let it be smoothly made, and well boiled. Put in a piece of sperm the size of a walnut, to 1 quart starch. [It is a good way to use the ends of candles, oil having become so high; it is cheaper and pleasanter to use them, even for "go-about" light, where there is gas.] The other articles in a wash do as well with a cheaper starch, made in the above manner. Collars may be made to look extremely well by sprinkling them down with the other clothes the evening before ironing, and, just as you iron them, dipping them, one by one, for a moment in cold water; wring and iron them—there will be a polish on them.

Another Way.—Put 2 oz. of gum arabic to 1 pint water; when dissolved, strain it through a cloth and bottle. Put 1 table-spoonful to each pint of starch after it is made. This gives lawns a new appearance: it makes laces and muslins stiffer. When you bottle the gum, put in a piece of corrosive sublimate the size of a pea, to prevent its becoming sour.

Ironing.—This has, through all time, been a wearisome, worrying process, at times, in the experience of all. The day has, I hope, nearly gone by, when "good fires" will be kindled and kept up, (perhaps through a whole day, while the thermometer ranges at 90,) just that a family ironing may be accomplished. In cities, where we have gas, an elastic tube is introduced into a flat iron made for the purpose; and at a cost of about four cents an hour, we have a perpetually heated flat iron. For those who have not gas, an equally pleasant spirit iron, with a wick lit by alcohol, performs the labour.

CLEANSING, ETC.

For Staining Floors, Piazzas, &c.—Make a strong lye of boiled wood ashes, add as much copperas as will stain the floor a light shade of oak: try a little first. Put on the wash with a mop dipped in the lye, and wet the boards well. When varnished, this lasts a season.

For Cleansing Brushes and Combs.— Put 1 tea-spoonful liquid ammonia into 2 quarts warm water; put in 1 brush at a time, rub it about quickly, dip it all over, rinse in clear tepid water, and wipe dry. Put in your combs several at once (as they are not varnished), and rinse and dry them; fine tooth combs thus cleansed, and just before using, cut a piece of white flannel the length of comb, and stick it through the whole length, about half-way up. Remove this when your hair is combed—will keep them so.

Ants.—The large black ants may be routed by a wet sponge, sugared: the small ones, by honey set about.

Soap for Mouse Holes.—A lump of hard soap is good to stop a rat, mouse, cockroach or ant hole. They all hate soap.

Several Methods of Cleaning Silver and Brass.—Cleanse silver with hot water: make a solution of equal parts of ammonia and spirits turpentine. Put it on with a soft cloth: while wet, have another cloth dipped in prepared chalk, or whiting, and go over the article: have a third clean dry cloth to polish.

Rotten stone and camphene are good, but the surrounding paint generally suffers if used on doors. The very best method is to wash the articles, whether gold chains, silver teapots or plated ware, in soft warm water, with 1 tea-spoonful liquid ammonia to $\frac{1}{2}$ gallon water; dry it, and have a leather dipped in rouge and burnish. A little rouge goes very far. Have a tooth brush for chased work.

There are also many good polishes sold in powders, under various names.

Another Method.—Dissolve a piece of alum the size of a shell-bark in 1 quart strong lye: scum it well, add soap, and wash the silver with it.—M. P.

Where the front door plates and knobs are cleansed every morning, a little fine whiting, with a soft rag, the breath blown a moment previously on it, keeps them bright, and saves paint and labour.

To take Stains out of Silver Plate.—Steep the plate in lye 4 hours: then cover it over with whiting wet with vinegar, a thick coat, and dry; after which rub off the whiting, and pass it over with dry bran, and the spots will not only disappear, but the plate will look exceedingly bright.

To Eject a Cork from a Bottle.—If the cork has been pressed into a bottle, take a strong twine and pass it in double; a little turning and the twine will enclose the cork, and so may be drawn out.

To Clean White Marble Mantles.—Brush them well with a brush, such as painters use, daily, and wipe with a soft dry towel. If soiled, dip a sponge in clean warm water and wash it, drying with a soft towel. To clean the carved part, wet a sponge with pumice stone, and gently rub on, washing off with pure water, drying with a towel: for the interstices, use a stick covered with a towel.

To Wash Oil Cloth.—Oil cloth may be made to have a fresh, new appearance, by washing it every month with a solution of sweet milk with the white of 1 beaten egg. Soap, in time, injures oil cloth. A very little "boiled oil" freshens up an oil cloth: very little must be used, and rubbed in with a rag. Equal parts of copal varnish I put; it gives a gloss.

To Red a Yard.—Many persons put red on a yard to cover green bricks. The green may be removed by pouring boiling water, in which any kind of vegetables (not greasy) have been boiled. Persevere in this a few days, and all green will disappear. For red colour, make a solution of 1 oz. common glue to 1 gallon water: while hot, put in alum the size of an egg, $\frac{1}{2}$ lb. venetian red, and 1 lb. or more Spanish brown. Try a little on a brick, let it dry, and add colour, if too light: water, if too dark.

To Wash Silk and Ribbons in Camphene.—Put a flat-iron to heat. Take 2 teacups, into which put 3 table-spoonfuls fresh pure camphene. Have an old tooth-brush, and a small planed board laid on a newspaper on the table. Lay the ribbon or tie-shawl along the board, wetting tooth-brush with the camphene, and rubbing it all over the article: hardest where it is most soiled: do this for a minute, turn over and do likewise: put it in the tea-cup used out of, pass it through your fingers to clean it, put it in the other tea-cup a minute; now have a clean cloth at hand, on which lay the ribbons. Have your ironing cloth ready, the iron just warm enough to pass rapidly over the silk. Iron it on both sides, when a few hours hanging in the air takes off all smell, and they resemble new ribbon. Do not iron your ribbon when it is too wet, but sop it a moment in the dry cloth, and it is ready.

Durable Ink.—100 grains lunar caustic, 1 drachm gum arabic, into 1 oz. soft water. *Preparation water.*—1 oz. sal soda, 2 oz. soft water: a little gum arabic to stiffen the linen.

How to Paper a Wall.—Cut off the right side of the pieces, measure one the height of the wall: cut up one piece in lengths, leaving any odd pieces for windows. Have a pine table, across which lay several of the lengths. Begin to paste by laying the one nearest you to the edge: paste it well all over: double it to within ½ yard of the top: carry it there, and have a clean towel over your shoulder: match the figure first at the ceiling, and use the cloth to smooth it as you pass your hand over the whole width: let the ends of the doubled part now fall, and keep on down smoothing as you go, till at the wash-board cut off the paper to fit snugly. When you wish to turn a corner, measure what is wanted: after wetting, cut the 2 ends a bit, and crease it between the ends on the edge of the table. Now you are ready for the border, when the room is covered. Cut it into lengths of 1½ yards, paste it, and go up the ladder with towel: be sure you are careful, matching it as it belongs.

Paste.—Mix wheat flour in a pail with tepid water. Pour boiling water on this, and it will thicken. Before you begin the room, paste at all the ins and outs of the wood-work little bits of the paper. For a *whitewashed* wall, make a solution of ¼ lb. glue to a gallon of water: boil it and put on with a whitewash brush.

Painting a Room.—Get a painter to mix the quantity of paint required. Purchase such a brush as is sold for 20 cents; have the surface you intend painting thoroughly cleansed from grease or spots; stir the paint well, and you can proceed. There is very little labor in this, and often may be done to advantage by a woman. If much of a job is undertaken, it is needful to have oil and turpentine added.

Economical Paint.—Skim milk 2 quarts, fresh slacked lime 8 oz., linseed oil 6 oz., white burgundy pitch 2 oz., Spanish white 3 lbs. The lime to be slacked in water, exposed to the air, mixed in one-fourth of the milk: the oil in which the pitch is previously dissolved, to be added a little at a time; then the rest of the milk, and afterwards the Spanish white. This quantity is sufficient for 27 square yards, 2 coats, and the expense not more than 25 cents.

Oxalic Acid will remove all stains from hands or clothing. But it must be used with great care, being not only a deadly poison, but tendering every fabric, if not wetted very soon.

For Rough Hands in Winter, rub pumice stone gently over them. (Sand soap is better.)

To Eradicate Roaches.—I know of but one method. Purchase a tin box of a sort of phosphorous paste, to be had only at Glentworth's, corner Race and Chester streets.

To Cleanse Carpets.—1 tea-spoonful liquid ammonia in 1 gallon warm water, will often restore the colour to carpets, even if produced by an acid or an alkali. If a ceiling has been whitewashed with carpet down, and a few drops are visible, this will remove it.

Another Way.—After the carpet is well beaten and brushed, scour with ox gall, which will not only extract grease but freshen the colours—1 pint of gall in 3 gallons warm water, will do a large carpet. Table floor-cloths may be thus washed. The suds left from a wash, where ammonia soap is used, even if almost cold, cleanses these floor-cloths well.

To Take out Fruit Spots.—Let the spotted part imbibe a little water without dipping, and hold the part over a lighted common brimstone match, at a proper distance. The sulphurous gas which is discharged, soon causes the spot to disappear.

To Preserve Pencil Drawings.—Lay them on the surface of skimmed milk: then take up one corner till it drains and dries. The milk must be perfectly free from cream, or it will grease the paper.

Renovation of Manuscripts.—Take a hair pencil, and wash the effaced part with a solution of prussiate of potash in water, and the writing will again appear, if the paper has not been destroyed.

Cleaning Prints.—Prints which have existed for years, and perhaps centuries, transmitted from hand to hand, passing through auctions, exposed in shop windows, turned over and over again in dealer's folios, necessarily acquire an accumulation of the dirt of ages; and yet may not have the ill-luck to be actually stained or soiled, otherwise than by this gradual effect of exhibition and use. In such cases, the chief part of the soiling thus acquired, may be removed by pure water merely. To effect this, the print is laid, face downwards, in a vessel large enough to admit of the whole paper lying quite flat; water boiling hot is then poured over it, sufficiently to cover it to the depth of an inch or more. The print is allowed to soak in the water, more or less time, according to circumstances. By degrees the dirtiness disengages itself from the surface into the water; the print is then taken out, and passed through fresh, clear water, and held or hung up, for the superfluous moisture to run from it: and, when this has sufficiently taken place, it is laid between sheets of white French blotting-paper, and covered by a thick mill-board, weights being laid on it, so as to have the effect of a moderate press; and it is thus left till dry. Where there is much soiling to be removed, and of old standing, it may be allowable to use, gently and carefully, a soft hair brush, while the print is saturated with the water, to assist in the disengagement of the impurities.

To Colour White Ribbons.—They should first be passed through water a little acid, to whiten them. For blue, put 1 oz. indigo into a bottle, with 3 oz. blue vitriol. Fill the bottle one-third full to allow for fermentation: leave out the cork. Let it stand 2 weeks before using: shake it once a day for a week, and if too thick add water.

This mixture, with warm water and alum, will colour any shade of blue in 5 minutes.

A little tumeric, mixed with boiling water and alum, colours any shade of yellow; scarlet lake and cream tartar, any shade of pink.

A few drops of blue mixed with the pink, makes dove colour.

To Mix Whitewash.—Pour a kettle of boiling water on a peck of unslacked lime; put in 2 lbs. whiting, and $\frac{1}{2}$ pint salt; when all are mixed together, put in $\frac{1}{2}$ oz. of Prussian blue, finely powdered; add water to make it a proper thickness to put on a wall.

Whitewash for Buildings or Fences.—Put in a barrel 1 bushel of best unslacked lime; pour on it 2 buckets of boiling water, and when it is mixed put in 6 lbs. fine whiting; fill up the barrel with water, stir it well, and keep it covered from the rain; let it stand several days before you use it, when stir it up; thin it with milk as you use it, and put $\frac{1}{2}$ a pint of salt to each bucketful. This makes a durable wash for a rough-cast or frame house, or for fences; the salt prevents it from peeling off.

To Extract Spots of Durable Ink.—A little sal-ammonia moistened with water.

To Clean Kid Gloves.—Use ammonia water, or burning fluid : keeping them on the hands, and rubbing till dry.

To Cleanse Rancid Pie Plates, and Earthenware, &c.—Boil them in lye, or a little saponifier made weak.

Sperm. Spots may be extracted with a knife : then lay soft paper, and place a warm iron over the spots : then rub them with brown paper.

To Extract Grease, Paint, &c.—For paint on cloth, fresh burning fluid rubbed in with a tooth brush takes away every trace, and leaves no smell : for silk, &c., it should be rubbed till dry, to prevent its leaving a stain.

Ants.—One of the "minor miseries" in our houses, is an army of ants. A chemist informs me they may be routed by making a solution of corrosive sublimate 1 oz., sal ammoniac 1 oz., water 8 oz. Mix and dissolve. Apply this with a hair pencil to all the places where they "most do congregate."

Flies.—It is all a mistake—the use of cobalt and fly paper, &c. They like it, eat it, and die; but scores of other flies come to the funeral, who else would not. It is far better, on pleasant days, to burn pepper, or any spice, on a shovel, in the room. They hate spices, and will flee.

Moths.—Drawers or wardrobes, where woollens are kept, should be occasionally emptied, and left open to the influence of fresh air and sunshine, and all the corners cleared from dust. This, and taking care never to put away clothes damp, will be most likely to prevent the moth. An empty whiskey barrel is said to be a preventive of the ravages of moth. Furs may have a few cloves sewed up in them.

Gas Burners.—Clean out *bat-wing* burners with the edge of letter paper: *fish-tail*, with a piece of broom corn.

Castor Bottles.—Put them half full of rice, and fill up with warm water; shake them well. This is the best method of cleaning pepper out.

USEFUL

AND

ORNAMENTAL WORK.

GRECIAN PAINTING.

This is a method of preparing mezzotint and aquatint engravings so as closely to resemble the finest paintings in oil.

DIRECTIONS.

1st.—Have made a pine frame, say two inches larger than the engraved part of the print.

2d.—Cut the engraving the size of the frame, then make a stiff paste and spread it thickly on the frame.

3d.—Place the engraving face down, sponge it gently with water, then press the frame firmly down on it—leave it until entirely dry, (not near the fire,) and it will become even and tight.

4th.—Pour sufficient spirits of turpentine on the back to moisten it well, then putting on the Grecian varnish, rub it thoroughly with your stiff brush, and continue to apply until perfectly transparent; after leaving it, if white spots appear, repeat the process.

Lastly.—Place it face down, where it will be free from dust, for two or three days.

Particulars, as to colors needed, as well as the other materials used, may be obtained of Scholz & Janentzky, 112 South 8th st., Philadelphia.

LEATHER WORK.

THE leather used for this purpose is called Blank Leather, by dealers. It can be had at any Leather and Morocco store, at from 50 to 75 cents a skin. The leaves or flowers are to be drawn with a black lead pencil on the smoothest side of the leather, and then cut out with a small pair of pointed scissors—they are then to be thrown into a cup of clear cold water until they are saturated with moisture, when they are to be laid on a towel, and are ready for being shaped or veined, according to the shape and veining of the leaf or flower they are meant to represent (but never, as you love nature, according to your fancy); use your ingenuity to the utmost in devising modes of imitating accurately, but do not try to invent other forms than her gracious hand supplies. Most leaves can be shaped by the finger, after the veins have been drawn upon the damp surface, which is best done with a rather blunt point of any thing almost—knitting needle or steel stiletto. Many flowers should be veined in the same manner, and most of them can be shaped by the finger—others, such as jasmin or convolvulus can be made cup-shaped, by pressing a round piece of leather into the mouth of a bottle, and drawing the edges down tightly over the lip of it—varying the size of the bottle to suit the size of the flower from the smallest homeopathic, up to any size required—they should be laid gently on a paper to dry, and are then ready for use.

To ornament frames of all kinds, for mirrors,

pictures, &c., for brackets, baskets, bonnets, &c., &c., they can be fastened on surfaces by nailing, sewing (which is best when possible) or gluing. The arrangement of them, for different purposes, gives room for the exercise of nice taste and discrimination; be careful to use the foliage proper to the flower, and do not surround grapes with rose leaves, nor jasmine with grape tendrils.

If intended to represent carved wood, they may be varnished, but they lose something of delicacy and beauty in the process.

The varnish should be best copal, applied with a camel's hair paint brush.

The easiest way to draw the outlines, is to cut the intended shape out of thin pasteboard, (a visiting card, for instance;) lay it on the leather and trace round it with a pencil.—E. W. T.

To make Twigs look like Coral.—Take clear rosin, dissolve it, and to every ounce of which add 2 drachms of the finest vermilion; when stirred well together, choose the twigs and branches, peeled and dried; then take a pencil and paint the branches all over while the composition is warm: afterwards shape them in imitation of natural coral. This done, hold the branches over a gentle fire till all is smooth and even, as if polished. White coral may be imitated with white lead, in the same manner.

To take Impressions of Medals and Coins, &c.—Melt a little isinglass glue with brandy, and pour it thinly over the medal, so as to cover its whole suface; let it remain on for a day or two, and then taking it off, it will be clear, and have an elegant impression of the coin. It will not soften in damp weather, as other glue.

Lamp Shades.—A variety of tasteful and beautiful shades may be made, by procuring large sheets of Bristol board, or fine map paper, cutting it the shape of the wire frame, making a scalloped edge and bottom, by placing a 25 cent piece on the edge and passing a pencil round it: then, when you have repeated this all along on both sides, cut half of the mark away. Now, with a shoemaker's punch strike holes in these scallops, and you are ready to make the wreath. Autumn leaves are elegant for this purpose : also, summer flowers. Sea weed has been used, and is very delicate and graceful. After putting on a few leaves, &c., with gum tragacanth, put large flat-irons on the work, and proceed. Some begin by painting a stem all across, and attaching the leaves, breaking off their stems. When you have completed the leaves, let them lie under pressure some hours. Cut coarse Tarlton muslin the shape, and with a little gum tragacanth, paste it to the scallops on both edges. Pare when dry. Join the shade carefully last, with gum, pressing it with a flat-iron.

Rustic Baskets.—Take a piece of wood four inches square; have four pieces the width of tape three inches long. Tack these to the middle of each side of this square, in an inclined position : drive a tack through the top of each of these uprights, take a piece of wire, pass it round these tacks and all around the basket, throw a handle over the top of the same, secure, and break it off; paint all green; when dry, put arbæ vitæ around inside, and on the handle, intersperse flowers, and you have a very pretty shaped extempore vase of flowers; if wet, it will last long. A piece of sponge, inserted below the flowers, keeps up moisture. A novel basket for cut flowers may be made by cutting a ripe sun-flower with quarter yard of stem, inverting it, placing a wet sponge below, flowers and green above, two or three toy birds and real butterflies down the handle; and, if you choose, varnishing the under part. It is then entirely water proof.

Picture Frames.—There are several ways of making inexpensive frames. One is to have a bookbinder's board cut into any form the picture demands, pasting dark paper or muslin over it, and using the Norway fir cones for covering. Shell the larger leaves off the cone, cut them smooth and glue them over the frame, to lie as the shingles of a roof—or with the points inner, and overlying each other. You may purchase wall paper imitating several woods, and paste neatly over a pine or other picture frame. When dry, varnish with two coats copal, and at a distance the illusion is almost complete. Toy cottages may be made in this way, of binders' board cut into cottage form, with deep gables, glass pasted inside for windows, papering the sides, &c.; then gluing on the roof, and afterwards the cones. Give two coats of copal varnish, when dry.

Moss Basket.—Procure the beautifully green hanging moss from trees. Make a shallow flanging basket of pasteboard: sew this moss within and without; keep it as a receptacle for the choice autumn gatherings of wood and field. It is very pretty.

Potichomania.—Potichomania is the art of giving glass the appearance of ornamented porcelain. Cut out carefully the designs which you wish to employ. Arrange them on a table as you wish them to appear in your Potiche. Apply with a brush some gum in the inside of the Potiche, over the whole surface you wish to fix your cutting; put in your cutting with care, and press every portion of it firmly to the glass, being careful to press out every particle of air. When your Potiche is entirely decorated, you will see that every thing is well secured; apply a coat of gum, and smooth down the paper; let it dry at least six hours, and again assure yourself that all is perfectly smooth; give the inside of the Potiche another thorough coat of gum; let it dry again, during at least 6 hours. It may then be painted any colour desired, by either pouring the paint into the Potiche, and running it around, or using a brush. If a second coat of paint should be desired, let the first become perfectly dry before the second is applied. When carefully made, as handsome vases can be produced as the imported, and at one-tenth the cost. All the materials may be procured of Scholz & Janentzky, Number 112 So. Eighth street. These vases cost from 20 cents to $5. Pictures, per sheet, from 25 cents to $2 50. Paint and gum, 25 cents per bottle. Brushes 25 cents. (See p. 127.)

Cottage Furniture—A number of inexpensive, convenient articles, may be made with a little ingenuity and calico, or mousseline, or moreen. If you have cane-seat chairs, which have become broken in the canes only, old merino or cloth may be tacked over, (putting thick muslin between,) then narrow gimping over the tacks. Give the chairs previously a washing in ammonia soap-suds, and a coat of copal varnish, and you have reno‑ vated them at little labour and cost.

For Seats.—If you have an old hair trunk, it may be converted into a pretty and useful seat, by covering it with merino or moreen; one on either side of a bed is useful for shoes and bonnets. You can get a neat table, and place for soiled clothes, by dressing a barrel with pink or blue chintz and lace over it, or furniture calico. Another way, is to get a carpenter to make you the frame for an hour-glass table. Dressed with furniture chintz, and pockets all round the top, it makes a very useful sewing table, for city or country.

A Divan.—An exceedingly useful couch may be had at small cost, by having a carpenter to make a frame of common stuff, 6 feet long, 28 inches wide, and 12 inches high. Have a sloping side-piece and head-piece cut out of a board: let the head-piece be 1 foot high, tapering to the whole width of couch: let the side-piece taper from the head: let this be 3 feet long. Have slats nailed across the bottom, or girth passed through holes bored in the sides. Let the side-piece and end be upholstered first, and nailed on: make a thick mattress of hay or straw for the bottom, and another of hair top. Cover with calico—a frill to reach the floor. There must be castors. One half of this divan may run under a bed, if the room is small. The best way to make a comfortable affair of it, is to let an upholsterer stuff it, and put in springs. This makes an additional cost of 3 dollars.

Bonnet Cases.—On leaving home, the transfer of a dress bonnet is often a difficulty. A neat article to carry a bonnet with caps inside of it, is made by cutting a thick pasteboard into a half circle, first cutting a paper pattern that shape, which will enclose the face : cut 2 of these alike : cut a strip deep enough to enclose the bonnet : try it by putting in your bonnet. Get dark quiet coloured glazed paper, baste it over the pasteboard, bind with ribbon the colour, make a lid to fit of the same, sew all together, and a loop or two, with button, will secure it from dust or wet. If you do not mind size, a bag of silk could be sewed to the top to hold any small light article, thereby avoiding the risk, in travelling, of losing small parcels.

Another way is to procure a square box, with lid ; make sides of Holland the height required for bonnet, have 4 pieces of wood the same height to stand in the corners, and you have a box which can be flattened at pleasure ; put into a trunk, and used at sea-side hotels, &c., where closets, &c., are not.

Making Shoes.—Women may make slippers and gaiters, by purchasing a last, and the implements sold at "Finding stores." Rip up an old gaiter ; cut out and make your uppers like it ; sew on tips of patent leather. Wet your sole, tack it wrong side out to the last, in three places. Tack the middle of your upper to the middle of instep of last, have a borer and a waxed end, and sew all round the shoe. When done, pound down the stitches with a hammer, turn the shoe, put it on the last again, pound the edges hard all round, and leave till dry. Next day you can make the other. Paste a linen sole lining ; or better, put in old thin soles, as the ones you make must necessarily be so. One can make satin or kid slippers very easily, at a most trifling cost: they will do for the parlour of an evening.

Making a Dress.—"Machine sewing" will do all parts of a dress, except button-holes; and you may make your own body linings fit, by ripping the baste out of one on which your dressmaker is at work, laying it on strong brown paper, cutting and creasing, just where her seems are, and next time doing it yourself.

Children's Toys.—It is interesting, when on a journey, or in the country, to gather moss, acorns, shells, sea grass, &c., and on returning have a cottage made of binders' board, and these glued or sewed on. They serve the double purpose of a remembrance for yourself, and a pleasure for children.

Toy Scrap Books.—It is well to save childish pictures, and wood-cuts of various kinds, (many of which give children an excellent idea of places,) and paste them into one of those large calico or worsted pattern books, which are called sample cards, and are of little use at the stores, after their season has passed. These books are lasting, and give much pleasure to children. Another way is, to select fancy-coloured muslin, then forming into leaves hemmed at the edges, upon which pictures may be pasted. Sew six of these together, and then join them. A stiff piece of pasteboard, covered with muslin, forms a nice binding.

DYES.

To Color Olive.—Make a strong sage tea, and add alum and copperas till it is dark: strain it: dip the article to be colored in soap suds, wring it out and dip it in the dye: wring it out, shake, and let it be aired a moment. If cloudy dip again in the dye. Maple bark and copperas make a good dark color.

Another Color.—Dissolve 1 oz. anotta in 5 gallons water: when boiling add ½ pint soft soap: the muslin must be wet in soap suds before putting in.

Yellow.—Boil peach leaves when they are turning yellow, in the autumn, with a little alum. Onion skins boiled with alum make a good yellow. Also a good yellow is produced by 1 table-spoonful turmeric in 1 pint water: make a strong lather of soap suds and boil the whole together. Dip as above.

Steel Color.—Tea grounds, set with copperas.

Pearl Color.—1 gallon boiling water, 1 teaspoonful pow. alum. Strain into this 1 gill good black ink. This makes a pearl color. A faded Shetland shawl may be renovated, by first washing it in a strong ammonia soap suds, and, after wringing, placing it in the above preparation. Let the air pass through it, after once wringing, and dip again. Now wring it very dry, and previously place newspapers on the floor of a room, then a large clean cloth, and spread and square the shawl upon it to dry, pinning it closely all around. Let it remain, till quite dry. A shawl so managed, looks exactly as well as a new one. Any color can be chosen: see "Dyes" in this book.

CEMENTS.

Cement for the Tops of Bottles or Jars. —Take equal parts of rosin and brick dust pounded fine, a lump of beeswax: stew them together, and keep in an old tin, melting it when you want to seal your bottles or jars.

To Stop Cracks in Iron Vessels.—Mix wood ashes and salt into a paste, with a little water: apply them, whether the vessels are cold or hot.

Cement.—3 parts ashes, 3 parts clay, and 1 sand, is said to make a cement as hard as marble, and impervious to water.

Liquid glue is good for vases, &c.

Loose handles of knives and forks may be refastened by making a cement of rosin and brick dust. Heat the handle, and pour in the cement very hot. Seal engravers do this.

Melt a little isinglass in spirits of wine, adding one-fifth water, and using a gentle heat; when perfectly melted and mixed it will form a transparent glue, which will unite glass so fast that the fracture will hardly be seen.

Cement for China.—Take plaster of Paris and mix it with liquid gum Arabic into a paste. This is said to be excellent.

Paste that will Keep.—Dissolve 1 oz. alum in 1 quart water warmed : when cold add as much flour as will make it the consistence of cream : then strew in as much powdered rosin as will lie on a dime, and the same of pow. cloves. Boil it to the proper consistency, stirring all the time. This will keep a year, and may be moistened with water, when dry.

A Mucilage that will Keep.—Take of powdered gum arabic 8 oz. ; sugar 1 oz. ; water 8 oz.; vinegar 4 oz.

Liquid Glue.—In a wide-mouthed bottle dissolve 8 oz. best glue in $\frac{1}{2}$ pint water, by setting it in a vessel of water, and heating, till dissolved. Then add slowly, constantly stirring, $2\frac{1}{2}$ oz. nitric acid. Keep it well corked, and it will be ready for use.

KNITTING, NETTING,

AND

CROTCHET.

(131)

A FEW RECEIPTS FOR KNITTING.

A Shawl.—Purchase 4 oz. of split zephyr, (some prefer the Shetland wool.) Get 1½ oz. of this, of some quiet colour, for border: the rest, white. Cast on 400 stitches (upon large needles) of the colour; narrow once in the middle of these stitches, which are all placed on 1 needle; narrow also at the end of every row; have your coloured zephyr divided into 4 parts; use up ¼ at first, then knit in as much white as you have coloured; then use the other ¼ of coloured, return to the white, and go on; it is better to put in a red string to note the middle, as the narrowing in the middle must be regular. You finish with 1 stitch; now ½ the shawl is made; begin, and do another like it. Sew them together, it does not show, and your job is far less burly and discouraging. A split zephyr shawl, 2 yards square, costs little over one dollar—a Shetland, half that. A coloured one made thus, of whole zephyr, would be strong and beautiful, but heavier. Small ties for head are made as above, casting on 150 stitches, and finishing the neck by taking up the loops and putting on a border all round.

Another.—A very pretty stitch for small work is made thus—Knit 1, knit 2 together: then draw the first stitch over the second, throw the thread over the needle: knit 3, throw the thread over the needle. Wrong side, heel. In the third round take care to knit for the 3 plain stitches, the 2 loops, with the narrowed stitch, between them.

Another.—Knit 3 plain stitches; draw the first

over the other two, throw the thread over the needle, knit three, draw the first over the second, and throw the thread over the needle. Wrong side, heel. In third round, put the hole in middle of the three plain stitches.

A Star Purse.—57 stitches on the needle, of green purse silk; knit 1 row, heel; second row, knit the first 3 plain, bind the first of these 3 over the other 2, put the thread in front of the needle, and so on, in the same manner. Change the colour to white, after every seam row.—M. A. B.

Mufflers.—Cast on 66 stitches of zephyr; rib it 2 and 1; knit thus for about 3 inches. Cast off, and net into the top 56 nets; go around the second time by putting 2 into one; make a few more, and finish.—M. M.

Gaiters.—Cast on 90 of dark or black tapestry; knit a few rows garter, and make holes for strings. (You do this by knitting two together, throwing over the thread;) put it into ribs, 2 and 2, narrowing every 9 rows at each end, till long enough to reach ankle; then divide the whole into 3 parts, leaving $\frac{1}{2}$ front, the rest on either side; put in another needle, cast on 46 stitches on the instep, and shape the front piece to your shoe, narrowing off at the side.

Infant's Socks.—Cast on 24 stitches on each 3 needles; rib 1, slip and bind; make 7, and knit 7 also; narrow 1 and rib; do this times enough to have 11 holes deep; put in coloured zephyr, rib every 5 rounds; make 5 ribs deep for heel, narrowing it as in a tiny stocking. When the heel is taken up, let there be narrowing to 38. Narrow 9 on the white instep before joining it to zephyr. Make 4 ribs before narrowing off toe, beginning with 6 and 6 between; let there be 20 holes from top to end of instep.—A. B.

A pretty quick-made Sock.—Cast on 31 stitches; knit 11 rows like garter, narrow and widen all across for holes; knit 2 rows more; knit 9 rows and bind off; commence at the back of sock, knit the 11, take up the 9 on instep, then cast on 11 at the end of needle; knit 9 more rows, narrow on the 10th, 11th and 12th; bind off. Commence at the toe and take up 11; take up 1 on instep, draw the 11th over 12th, leaving 11; knit 9 rows across, take up the 9 on the opposite side: then knit the 11 rows, then the 9; narrow on the 10th, 11th, 12th. Bind off.—M. E.

A Round Guard.—Cast on 4 stitches; knit them, then slip them to the other end of needle, and pull the first stitch tightly. This makes a round string, and soon done.

For Knitting Shoes.—Cast on 24 stitches, 3 rows thrown up and 4 knit plain, for 31 ribs. Throw on 24 for the instep, finishing the toes with 19 ribs. Commence narrowing the 4th rib from the instep, narrow once at each end of the needle on every plain row, for 3 rows; then narrow every plain and every rib until it is small enough, leaving 27 stitches at the end. Take up the stitches at the top for the edge, according to fancy. 1 oz. of worsted for a pair of shoes.

Directions for Knitting an Infant's Cap.—Cast 45 stitches of double zephyr on a wooden needle; knit 4 times across the needles; then slip off the first stitch, turn the zephyr twice round the needle, and knit two together; continue this to the end of the needle, then 4 times across; then the narrowing and widening row, or the zephyr wound twice round the needle, and the stitches, after you knit 4 rows of holes, and 4 plain rows, then take 10 stitches off each end of the needles, and tie them up to prevent them running down; then knit the remaining 25 stitches with the 4 plain rows, and the row of holes between; on the third row of holes narrow 1 stitch, on the middle of the needle; on the fourth row of holes, narrow 1 stitch on the middle of the needle; on the fifth row of holes, narrow 2 stitches on the middle of the needle; on the sixth row of holes, narrow 2 stitches on the middle of the needle. Then knit 3 rows of plain knitting, when you come to the end of the third row; then take up the stitches along the side of the crown and knit up the 10 stitches you tied up; then knit back, and take up the stitches on the opposite side of the crown, and the 10 stitches you tied up; then knit a row of holes, and 4 plain rows; continue this until you arrive at the sixth row of holes, when you widen 1 stitch on each side of the needle; then widen two stitches on the seventh needle, widen 3 stitches on the eighth row of holes, and widen 4 stitches on the ninth row of holes; then knit 4 rows of holes, and the 4 plain rows between—4 plain rows complete the cap. Put cotton in the hem.

Wash Mitten.—Cast on 50 of No. 8 tidy cotton: make it ¼ yard long, narrowing 4 or 5 times at the end of last rows. Sew it up, all but a thumb-hole.—E. N.

Tidy Edging.—Cast on 9: knit the first 3 stitches plain, leaving 6 at the left end: turn in the cotton, knit 2 together, do again and again : turn in the cotton, and the 2 last, plain : next row plain : continue the above till 9 holes are made; then knit 2 plain rows between, and reverse it, by narrowing after the first stitch is knit, where you widened before, and throw over the thread just as above.—M. E.

Chair Tidy.—Cast on 117 stitches : knit the first 3 rounds like a stocking : slip the first stitch loosely, narrow the next 8 to 4 : make a stitch, knit a stitch, and so on till there are 7 made stitches : make a stitch, narrow 1, and go on as it is commenced : knit 3 rounds between this. Get No. 8 cotton—$\frac{1}{4}$ lb. makes 2.

Honey-comb Stitch.—Knit 3 rows so as to be all pearled (or heeled) on the right side : then slip off 2, and knit 3 all across : do this 5 times in succession : then again pearl the 3 rows, knitting all the stitches, when these 3 rows are made. There will be occasional widening or narrowing needful in this stitch, at the end of needle, as it is not right without there are 3 on the end, when commenced with 3; or narrowed to 2, when 2 is the commenced number. Upon beginning every other figure, you must reverse it, as above said. This makes a rich bureau or table cover, but is tedious.—L. A. S.

Lily Bell.—6 plain, 4 seamed between them, go all across : begin by seaming 4 ; then cast on 6, knit 4, seam, and so on across. Do this for 9 rows : then narrow each side of bell till there is but 1. Begin another row of bells by seaming 4 : cast on 6, as above : then seam 1, narrow 1. and there are 4 between, as above. Go on in this way till the toilet cushion is done. This is a very beautiful stitch.

Wool Undersleeves.—Cast on 60 stitches with coarse steel needles : rib it 2 and 2, for 20 rows : then put in wooden needles : make 10 rows of these : put in the steel ones again, make 10 ribs : do. 3 of these : do. 4 between : make 12 ribs to finish. Sew them up.

For Knitting Pitcher Purses.—Set on 8 stitches to form 8 points : knit a round plain, then another, throwing the silk before the needle at each stitch. The next plain, putting on 8 beads, which must be pulled through the stitch on to the right side. The next widen again 8 times, then a plain round with 2 beads at each point, and so on, until 9 heads are on. Now you are done widening. Then another plain round, and another of 9 beads : when you begin to decrease, 2 at every point, till it is finished.

Knit 2 plain rounds before beginning purse stitch, putting on 2 beads at once, every other one, so as to form diamonds, until 20 rows are knit : then 2 rows of beads round and round, knitting a plain round after each. Rib 2 and 2 to form the neck, 26 rounds : then take off 6 stitches for the handle to form the spout ; knit backwards and forwards ; take off 2 stitches at the end of the needle till but 18 remain, narrowing twice every other round as the beginning of each needle, just as you finish. Knit to the place for the handle, make 6 stitches ; then a plain round, a row of beads, another plain round, another row of beads, and then take them off. For handle knit the first stitch, then put on 5 beads, slip to the other end of needle, and a plain row, and so on till long enough. Put on the ring and sew just below the 2 rows; sew up the side; put a tassel on the bottom.—M. A. C.

To Knit a Boy Doll.—Of zephyr ½ oz. for jacket : ½ oz. for pants : 3 skeins for cap—3 flesh colour, 2 black, 1 white. Set on 35 stitches for the pants : knit 20 rounds plain. Narrow alternately at each end of needle. Narrow 4 times, knitting 3 rounds between each. Narrow 7 times, knitting 2 rounds between each. Narrow every round till there are 18 stitches. Take 9 stitches, and join on the white zephyr; knit 1 row plain, the next seam, till there are 11 rows. Join the black to the other 9, and knit 7 rounds for the heel. Take up 8 stitches on each side, and narrow every other round till there are 10 stitches. Knit as long as the white, and then knit round and round, one round seam and one plain, narrowing off at the toe. Knit 2 of these, sew each one up separately as far as it is narrowed, and join them together by the other part.

For the jacket set on 70 stitches; knit 4 rounds for the polka; knit this to the top of the pants, with 4 needles: knit 1 row plain, the next seam, and so on. Narrow 4 on each side to form the hips; knit 18 rounds, then divide in half, and 8 rounds will form the arm-hole. To form the shoulders, narrow 1 at each end of the needle, till there are 14 stitches. Take up 6 stitches at the top of the arm-hole, and widen by throwing the thread before the beginning of the needle, till there are 24 stitches. Knit 13 rounds. Narrow 6 times, knitting 2 rounds between each. Narrow every round till there are 12 stitches. Head-knit 5 rows to the thumb, widening 2 under it. Take 4 middle stitches, and knit on 2 needles, like guard chain, 7 or 8 rows. Knit 2 or 3 rows, and then knit 4 fingers like the thumb. Head-knit on 4 needles 6 or 8 rows; widen 4 under the mouth; widen 1 on each side behind, till there are 54 stitches. Knit plain up to the top of the nose, then take 3 stitches with 2 other needles, and widen by throwing the thread before the needle, till there are 8 stitches; 8 or 9 rows make it long enough. Take up the 3 stitches at top of nose, and knit round 6 rounds till high enough for the forehead. Work the eyes, cheek and mouth, with suitable colours; then stuff with cotton. Hair is knit with 5 stitches plain, and binding off 2; press it with a wet cloth, and unravel the other 3; 2 or 3 rows of this sewed on the back of head.

The cap, set up 50 stitches; knit 4 rounds, and then narrow one at each end of needle till none left; sew up and trim with cord. Or a crotchet cap is pretty. Collar: 40 stitches, 5 or 6 rounds; then a strip for the front of jacket, 32 stitches, 4 rounds, and knit on it, and 6 buttons put on it.—M. A. C.

Polish Boots.—Cast on 380 stitches: rib 3 and 2: do this straight till 3 inches are made: then narrow in the middle rib every time on either side until 8½ inches are made: now cease narrowing, and make it as much longer as you choose.

Bedstead Drapery.—2 lbs. No. 8 tidy cotton divided into 4 parts: cast on 70 stitches with wooden needles, No. 00. Knit it in garter stitch till one part of the cotton is used up: cast it off: then knit three others likewise. Purchase ball fringe sufficient for one side of each piece; also cord and tassels of white cotton, for the places where the 4 pieces are joined and gathered into a space of about 12 inches, viz., in the centre of each side of the cornice, and baste the knit drapery upon it holding it somewhat loosely upon the tape. Secure it with pins to another tape tacked on the cornice.

NETTING.

This is convenient for pick-up work, or parlour, evening or conversation work; the operation being only mechanical, and not requiring much sight or attention.

A Shawl.—60 loops cast on: 2 rows of a colour, using 6 shades of zephyr: the same number of white, make 10 stripes for centre. For the border in the first row put 3 loops in each mesh: on the fourth and fifth from the point behind, put 3 in each mesh: then the first, second and third from point, put 4 in each mesh: in the point, put 5. At the commencement of each row of the border widen 1. This shawl takes 7 oz. tapestry; the centre one has a mesh three-fourths of an inch deep: that which goes round last but one, being two and a half do.

A Very Elegant Tidy—Is made by casting on 60 loops, and narrowing down to 1; break it off and begin at the 60, tapering off that side. The mesh used first row should be a degree less in size, to allow for the loop being removed. If 40 sewing cotton is used, and the tidy darned in figures or flowers, you have a lace-like affair.

Bottle Stand.—Put on 25, with a mesh the size of a dress whalebone: 6 rows of these; then put two into every one, and make 10 rows; then do not widen, but put in a large mesh; make 16 rows with 8 shades—1 row of each shade, and reverse it; finish it off as you commenced. This made of green, shaded, is moss-like and beautiful.

A Tidy, which has an unusual effect, may be made by netting straight along (the size you wish), with a small whalebone, and every row missing 1 loop, and taking and netting the next: being careful to alternate at the beginning of row. It is best to put in a red mark, which you did last. Use 40, spool cotton.

CROTCHET.

It is impossible to enumerate the beautiful and useful articles which may be made with this little implement—the crotchet needle. It is peculiarly convenient—takes up no room, and mostly can be when and where no other work would be admissible. It may be made to fill up those tedious "waiting" moments known to all our experience.

A Table Cover.—Procure $\frac{1}{2}$ lb. No. 8 tidy cotton: cast it on by making a chain of 5, linking it, widening as for a mat, and putting in any patterns to form a variety. These are pleasant beneath a gas-burner, and either save a costly cover, or hide a shabby one.

Crotchet Bonnet.—5 spools, No. 8 crotchet cotton; begin at crown, widen till 14 rounds are completed; then do 9 plain rounds; then widen 1 in every 10, on the tenth round; then put in a black thread to mark the middle of the back. There must be 12 stitches left in the middle of back, and the thread begun on the right side—commencing the first 3 or 4 stitches in single crotchet, break off the thread at the end of the rows. Begin next row 2 off from the last, stopping do.: do this 7 times, which gives slope enough for the neck. Now the face is to be begun, by beginning at the first stitch and widening 1, also at the last: break off the thread each row: do this while making 18 rows. You are now ready for finish of face and cape. Crotchet all round the bonnet 10 times, widening once in every 10 stitches on each row; also, when you come to the ears, doing all behind single crotchet. The bonnet is double, and looks more chip-like made on wrong side. This bonnet can be done up at home to look well. Borrow a block from your milliner, first putting the bonnet in the wash, then starching stiffly and rough-dry: save some of the starch, and when dry dip again, and rough-dry. Then have the block ready, put the bonnet in clear cold water a moment, wring it out dry and block it, putting pins at the ears and ends. Set in a chair in the sun, throwing a lace over it to save soil, while drying.

Another, open work.—Cast on 4 loops, widen for 18 rows: then do 20 rows without widening: then drop 17 loops and do 32 rows, widening at each ear: then 4 rows all round the bonnet, (save just behind:) then 1 round the face of larger loops.—C. S.

A very pretty finish to crotchet table covers and cake tidies is, to make a chain of 5: then make a bag in single crotchet large enough to hold a cherry stone; put it in and work over it.

Crotchet Shawl.—5 oz. Shetland wool: cast on a chain as long as you wish the shawl in size. Put 4 double crotchet into 1: leave 2 between, and repeat this all across: next row do the very same into the centre of the 4 double crotchet stitches all across. You will find a very coarse needle will make the work more open and elegant. Crotchet all round any pattern you wish, in any colour. Here is a useful shawl for 62 cents.

HINTS FOR MAKING A CITY GARDEN.

MANY of the yards in cities are small, and not much visited by the sun. By a little attention, even a shady yard with "moss-covered" bricks, may be made to show other signs of verdure than this, by planting such shrubbery as will not only bear the shade, but do better there. To remove the green from bricks, as well as directions for reddening them, see page 109.

The garden implements needed, are—a light hoe, a garden trowel, a watering pot, and a variety of seeds, roots and bulbs, which can be obtained at any of the florists'.

Prepare the soil, if clayey, by putting on a covering of sand 3 inches deep, and the same depth of well-rotted manure. Spade it in as deep as possible, and mix it well. Ashes are good for all kinds of soil, as they loosen those which are close, hold moisture in those that are sandy, and destroy insects. The best kind of soil is that which will hold water the longest, without becoming hard when dry.

For Pot Plants.—Take one-fourth common soil, one-fourth well-decayed manure, and half vegetable mould from the woods. Break up the manure, sift it through a coarse sieve, mix the materials thoroughly.

Planting Seeds.—Never plant when the soil is very wet. When the seeds are small many should be planted together, that they may assist each other in breaking the soil. Never water with **very**

cold water. It is best to plant seeds at two different times, lest the first should fail, owing to wet or cold weather.

Transplanting.—Transplant at evening, or just before a shower. Set them a little deeper than before, and press the soil firmly round them. Water and cover them a day or two. If the soil just around has not been removed, transplanting retards but little.

To Re-pot House Plants.—Renew the soil every year, soon after the time of blossoming. Prepare soil as above. Loosen the earth from the pot by passing a knife round the sides. Turn the plant upside down; remove the pot, and remove all the matted fibres at the bottom, and all the earth except that which clings to the roots. From woody plants, like roses, shake off all the earth. Take the new pot and put a piece of broken earthenware over the hole at the bottom, and then hold the plant in a proper position, shake in the earth around it. Now pour in the water to settle the earth, and heap in fresh soil till the pot is full. Small pots are better than large ones, as the roots are not so likely to rot from excess of moisture.

Bulbs, &c.—Plant the crocus in 10th mo. (Oct.); cover 2 inches deep and 4 apart. Hyacinths at the same time, 8 inches apart and 3 or 4 deep, in a rich soil. Jonquils at the same time, 2 inches deep. These should not be taken up oftener than once in 3 years. Narcissus also, in this month, 4 inches deep, covered with straw and leaves through the winter, and uncovered the middle of 3d mo., (March.) Plant tulips in rich soil at this time, 3 inches deep. Plant tube roses late in the 4th mo., (April,) in a rich soil. They are delicate and should be covered, in case of frosts. Daffodils should be planted 2 inches deep. Bulbs, in glasses, must have the water changed every week.

When they have done flowering, they should be dried, and put in a dry place till 10th mo., (Oct.,) when they are to be re-planted, taking off the off-sets, and putting them in a bed by themselves.

Annuals.—These should be so planted that the tallest may be behind, and flowers of similar colour should not be near each other. Many of one kind are prettiest together.

Verbenas.—These flowers are now very popular. It is best to plant them out in 4th mo., (April,) watering them in dry weather, and they will flower profusely, lifting some of the plants before frost, for winter flowering. They ought to be allowed to run according to their nature, for if tied up, they will not do so well, being in that way much exposed. The purple kind, left out, will survive the winters of Philadelphia.

Pot Plants.—The best situation for plants, in pots, is to shade them from the sun, and fully exposed to the air while blooming. Myrtles and Oleanders are very subject to the white scaly insect, and before the heat of summer begins they should be well cleansed.

Plants coming into Flower.—Examine the beds and keep down the weeds. A garden well kept is easily kept. Paint green all the sticks which are to be used as props. Sixpence worth of green paint refreshes thrice its cost.

Daisies may be planted out in shady places: the

sun destroys them during summer, if exposed. Hydrangeas do well in the shade, and will bloom in summer, even if left out in the winter.

Climbers.—The most beautiful perennial climbers are sweet-scented monthly honeysuckle, white, yellow, and coral do., clematis, purple glycene and pea.

Annual Climbers.—The most desirable are white and buff thunbergia, morning glory, red and white cypress. The latter two are very pretty, planted thickly round the bare trunk of a tree, and trained upon strings to the branches above; planted in a line, and trained on a net, these two vines look well also.

Scarlet sage, snowberries and chrysantheums pay better for their keep, than almost any other products of our city gardens—coming after nearly all other flowers have gone, and bearing slight frosts, if covered at nightfall.

Roses.—Roses in a garden are "a joy forever." The most desirable for cities, are—the grevillie, which will bear any Philadelphia winter: the tea, which, with a slight protection, will also: the daily, than which no rose is hardier: the moss, somewhat difficult of culture, if not in a rich sandy soil; but if fairly established in a rich deep loam, its permanency is sure: the prairie rose, "whose constitution is such," says Buist, "that it will bear the icy breezes of the St. Lawrence, or the melting vapours of the Mississippi." It is adapted for covering rock-work, old buildings, &c. It also delights in a procumbent posture, and can be used to make a flowery carpet of every shade of colour. Last, but not least, I can recommend the hermosa as being most desirable. The exquisitely cupped form of the flower, blooming on and on, through the autumn, renders it a perfect charm round a cottage, or in a city yard.

These varieties may be obtained of H. A. Dreer, 327 Chestnut street.

Grape Vines.—Every one can, with ease, have a rich supply of grapes. A grape vine is ornamental, even without its fruit. But a few feet of ground are needed—under a window, beside a door or lattice, in a corner of the yard, close under a fence: or, if in the country, near the roots of some old stump or tree, or on some hill-side, amid rocks and ledges, where, for other purposes, the ground is useless; on the bank of some dancing brook, or down on the sunny side of some old rock, where beneath its grey mossy side gushes forth a spring of crystal water, near which the grape almost always does well. Many kinds of them are so easily cultivated, and so hardy, that it seems wrong to find a dwelling without one.

The Isabella, Catawba and Elsinburg, best repay culture. Previous to planting the vines, care should be taken that the ground be well prepared for some distance around, for the roots to spread. The soil should be deep and dry, and some rich compost, or vegetable mould, should be used around the roots in filling in: a handful or two of wet ashes may be added: plant in 3d mo. (March.) It has been proved repeatedly, that the best manure for vines, is the branches pruned from the vines themselves, cut into small pieces, and mixed with the soil by means of a garden hoe. Dr. Liebig mentions several instances of vines being kept in a thriving condition for from ten to thirty years, by the trimmings of vines alone. If guano is used, 4 lbs. to 33 gallons of water is quite strong enough. A very good manure for vines is said to be made by saving all the leaves, and digging them in. In the vicinity of Philadelphia, a southern exposure is best. There are various methods of training and pruning the vine: it having a tendency to produce its most vigorous shoots at the extremities of the branches, and particularly so at those which are situated highest; it generally happens when it is trained high, that the greater portion of the fruit is borne near the top: and the fruit produced on the vigorous shoots is generally more abundant, and of finer quality than that produced on the short lateral ones, from which circumstance high training seems best calculated for city gardens. It is said that ripe grapes, gathered in dry weather, if placed between layers of cotton, and kept at a temperature just above the freezing point, will keep till spring.

Apples, Pears and Peaches.—Having visited an orchard near Philadelphia, where the yield of fine apples and peaches was wonderful, I was induced to inquire the method of culture. The owner (Edward Garrett) informed me, that in the spring he bathes the trunk, and far into the branches, with soft soap thinned with lye. When the late frosts (which destroy the peach blossoms in so many parts of our country,) touch the opening flowers, he sprinkles plaster upon these flowers, carefully going over the whole orchard. These peach trees have been in fine bearing for 10 years! He finds that corn and potatoes do well in this orchard, while wheat, sown in a corner of it one season, he believes was the means of killing several fine peach trees.

Garden Vases.—Purchase the earthenware garden vases, which may be had at the principal potteries; paint them several coats of white, marbling at the last, if you like it, and you have vases which are just as beautiful as the costliest ware.

Another.—Take empty kegs in which white lead comes, have two colours paint ready, (one white,) paint the hoops on both ends white, and half the staves alternately; when three coats of this are dry, paint the other staves drab or green: drab is prettiest; and you have a neat garden tub, which, in the country, has a pretty effect, and serves either for plants, or as a receptacle for weeds, which may be pulled up about the grounds.

The wire and iron garden furniture, are great embellishments to our city yards: from the grape-vine arbour to the flower stand and cypress trainer: while the iron sofas add much to comfort and beauty. Very elegant articles in this line may be had at N. E. corner Sixth and Market streets.

Rock Work.—This has a very pleasing effect in our city yards, especially if a fountain be the central ornament. There is, in Philadelphia, a most refreshing one, where the water, dripping over and through the rock work, moistens and keeps alive a variety of mosses and ferns gathered from interesting localities in Europe. These rockeries are made by arranging stones or rocks in such shapes as will be agreeable to the eye, leaving room between them for the growth of ferns, climbers, mosses, and other **plants, which naturally flourish among rocks.**

MISCELLANEOUS.

Dentrifices.—White's Tooth Powder is very good. The common strawberry is said to be a natural dentrifice, and its juice dissolves the tartar and makes the breath agreeable. Honey and charcoal make a good dentrifice.

To Prevent Corns.—Wear easy shoes: frequent bathing the feet in warm water, with a little salt, or potash, dissolved in it. The corn itself may be completely destroyed by rubbing it daily with a little caustic solution of potash. Lunar caustic, touched with a hair pencil, night and morning, also is good to cure corns.

To Remove Warts.—Sal ammoniac will remove them; also, lunar caustic.

For a Weak Back.—Take a beef's gall, pour it into 1 pint alcohol, and bathe frequently. It acts like a charm.

Cure for Corns.—Bind a piece of sponge, moistened in a weak solution of pearlash, on going to bed. It is said that the skin may be brushed off in the morning, having been dissolved by the action of the caustic. I have been entirely cured by a poultice of bread and water, with a little laudanum and paregoric put in, putting it on 2 nights at bed-time.

Another Cure.—Take equal parts pulverized indigo, common brown soap and tallow: of these make a soft ointment, by rubbing well together.

Spread it on soft leather and apply: keep it on till relieved.

Court Plaster.—Put 4 beeves' feet into a large quantity of water: let them boil until the meat will leave the bone: then take them out, skim the oil carefully off, put the liquor on again in a smaller vessel, and boil it till it is of a suitable consistence to spread on silk (say the thickness of molasses) with a brush.

Cold Cream.—Take $\frac{1}{2}$ oz. white wax, do. of spermaceti, and 3 oz. of almond oil. Put the whole into a basin, and place it in hot water till fused :. then gradually add 3 oz. rose water, elder water, or orange flower water, stirring all the time with a fork or small whisk. When cold it is fit for use. —A. M. M.

For Colouring Sea Weed Red.—Dip the moss into a boiling solution of 1 oz. alum in 1 pint water. Dry it. Make a solution of $\frac{1}{4}$ oz. cochineal, $\frac{1}{4}$ oz. cream tartar, one table-spoonful spirits hartshorn to $\frac{1}{2}$ tumbler water. Dip in the moss, wring, and dry in the shade.

Crystallized Grasses.—9 oz. alum dissolved in 1 pint water. Put in the grass when the alum water is cool enough to bear the hand; watch it, and take it out when the crystals are large as you wish: dry them on paper. If you wish colours, get a few powdered paints and sprinkle over, directly it comes from the water: heat alum over when it becomes cold.—M. L. N.

Ink in Books.—Oxalic acid will remove blots.

A Very Celebrated Cologne Water.—
6 drachms of oil of lemon, do. bergamot, 3 do. lavender, 10 drops cinnamon, 20 drops of cloves, $\frac{1}{2}$ drachm rosemary, 40 drops neroli, 20 drops rose, 2 drachms tincture of musk, 6 pints deodorized alcohol. Shake up well; let it stand 4 hours before filtering.

Stains in Table Linen.—Tie up cream tar. at the spot, and then put to boil in cold water.

Another Way.—Hold the part over a lighted match.

Bandoline.—Pour over 1 oz. quince seeds 1 pint of boiling water. Let it stand over night; next morning slightly boil it and strain it; when cold, add 4 table-spoonfuls of alcohol, and 2 or 3 of cologne, and flavor it with the oil of almonds, or whatever you prefer.—M. E. W.

Indelible Ink, without Prepara. Water.
$1\frac{1}{2}$ drachms nitrate silver; 1 oz. soft water; $\frac{1}{2}$ oz. strong mucilage gum arabic: mix these in a bottle, and keep in a dark place till dissolved, and ever after. For use, shake the bottle, then dip a clean quill pen in the ink, and mark: hold it close to the fire, or pass a warm iron over it, and it will become indestructible by time or acids.

CONTENTS.

	PAGE
PREFACE	3
BREAD, BISCUIT, AND WARM CAKES	5
BREAKFAST RELISHES	13
FISH	19
SOUPS	21
MEATS, POULTRY, ETC	23
SIDE DISHES	30
VEGETABLES	33
SAUCES	39
PICKLES AND CATSUPS	40
SPICED SWEET PICKLES	44
SALTING MEATS	44
TEA RELISHES	46
CAKES	49
FLAVOURS	56
PASTRY	56
PUDDINGS, AND DESSERTS	59 & 97
JELLIES, ETC	68
PRESERVES	71
SYRUPS	81
PLEASANT DRINKS	82
WINES	81
GAS COOKING	83
NURSING THE SICK	85
COOKERY FOR THE SICK	85
WINTER AND OTHER STORES	93
USEFUL IMPLEMENTS	98
HINTS FOR WASHING AND IRONING DAYS	101
CLEANSING, ETC	107
USEFUL AND ORNAMENTAL WORK	117
GRECIAN PAINTING	118
LEATHER WORK	119
CEMENTS	129
KNITTING, NETTING, AND CROCHET	131
HINTS FOR MAKING A CITY GARDEN	146
MISCELLANEOUS	153

INDEX.

	PAGE
Acid, Oxalic	112
Apples, Iced	61
Tapioca	62
Float	62
Crab	76
to Keep	95
Apple Tapioca	97
Apples, Preserved	99
Apples	151
Ants, to Kill	115
Annuals	148
Arrow Root	89
Asparagus	33
Bark, Slip, Elm	85
Baskets, Rustic	111
Bandoline	100
Barley Water	89
Basket, Moss	121
Bedstead Drapery	139
Beer, Penny	82
Ginger	82
Horehound	83
Beef, Frizzled and Liver	16
Hashed	22
Boileau	24
Alamode	24
Roast	24
Steak	17
Pickled	44
Beets	37
Beans, String	34
Lima	35
Pickled	43
Biscuit, Milk	8, 9
Tea	50
Blancmange in Eggs	70
Bleaching Liquid	104
Blackberries	89
Blackberry Syrup	89
Broth, Mutton and Beef	88
Liebig's, for sick	90
Bonnet Case	124
Bread, Moist	142
Wheat	6
Rye and Bran	7

	PAGE
Butter	7
Drawn	39
To cure	8
Buns, Philadelphia	51
Burlington	51
Buena Vista	51
Spanish	55
Bulbs	147
Burns, Cold Water for	90
Cake, Soda	10
Batter	10
Flannel	10
Buckwheat	11
Buttermilk	11
Corn Batter	12
Cornmeal	12
without Eggs	12
Lady	50
Golden	50
Silver	50
Poor Man's	51
Cocoa Pound	51
Bread	51
Cocoa-nut	21
Sponge	52
Grafton	52
Albany	52
Meat	30
Pound	52
Cup	53
Queen	53
Black	53
1, 2, 3, 4	54
Kisses	54
Jelly	54
Scotch	54
Loaf	54
without Eggs	54
Crullers	53
Calf's Head	27
Cauliflower	36, 40
Carrigen	66
Cabbage, Boil	36
Calicos, to wash	104
Cap, Infant's	134

INDEX.

	PAGE		PAGE
Candy, Molasses	70	Divan	124
Cans, Self-Sealing	77	Dolls, Boy	130
Carbonated Drink	82	Door Knobs	99
Carpets, Cleansed	112	Doughnuts	54, 55
Carrots	36	Dress, Make	120
Cocoa-nut Custard	60	Drawings, to Preserve	113
Pudding	60	Dressing	39
Corn Oysters	32	Dumplings, Drop	23
Chocolate, Cocoa	13	Ducks, Roast	29
Charlotte Russe	65	Dye, Steel Color	127
Cranberries	75	Pearl	127
Crotchet	143	Yellow	127
Cements	129		
Cherry Vinegar	81	Edging, Tidy	135
Cherries, Sweet Pickled	44	Eggs, Boiled	14
Chocolate	13, 86	to Keep	96
Chops, Mutton	27	Egg Plant	16, 38
Cheese Head	18	Extracts, Cooking	143
Chapped Hands	143		
Lips	90	Fish, Rock	19
Chickens, Fricassee	26	Fry Fresh	20
Broiled	26	Boil	20
Salad	46	Forcemeat Balls	28
Pie	57	Flavors, Peach and Rose	56
Cinnamon Loaf	50	Floating Island	64
Clams, Fried	27	Flour, Patent	10
Climbers	149	Flummery, Rice	67
Clothes' Dryer	104	Floors, &c., staining	107
Corns, to Prevent	153	Flies	115
Court Plaster	154	Fowls, Boiled	26
Cottage Furniture	123	Fricassee	31
Cologne	100	Fritters, Clam	16
Corn, to Keep	93	Corn	16
Coffee	85, 14	Stale Bread	63
Cork, from a Bottle	108	Snow	67
Coral Twigs	120	Fruit, Frosted	75
Combs, Cleansing	107	Furniture, Polish	142
Corn, Green, to Boil	34		
Fricassee	34	Gas Burners	116
Cookery for the Sick	85	Cooking	84
Croquettes	32	Gaiters, to make	133
Cream, Ice	66	Garden, to make	146
Snow	66	Gingerbread, Hard	50
Whipped	67	Mountain	49
Cold	154	Gingerbread Nuts	49
Cutlets, Veal	28	Goose, Roast	28
Cucumber, Pickled	40	Grecian Painting	118
Custard Apple	60	Gruel, Corn	88
Cold	63	Oatmeal	88
Cocoa-nut	60	Grasses, Crystallize	154
Frozen	66	Grape Vines	150
A. H.'s	66	Gravy, Turkey	22
Boiled	86	Gutta Percha	127
Custard Pudding	63	Guard, a Round	134
Crullers	53	Gloves, to Clean	115
Dentifrices	154	German Puffs	97

INDEX.

	PAGE
Ham, Fried	16, 29
Bake or Boil	27, 32
Hams, Salt	45
Premium	45
Hamlin Cake	100
House Plants, Re-pot	147
Hominy, Boil	53
Fry	34
Halibut, Fried	31
Icing	55
Ironing	106
Iron Holders	142
Ink, Durable	110
Iced Grapes	98
Ice Cream	98
Ink Stains	153
Indelible Ink without Prep. Wa	154
Jam, Quince	70
Jelly, Calves' Foot	68
Gelatine	69
Tapioca	68
Current	69
Apple	69
Rice	69
Quince	69
Jumbles	50
Cocoa-nut	52
Ketchup, Tomato	43
Knitting, Netting, &c	131
Lamp Shades	121
Limes, Preserved	73
Laundry Iron	142
Leather-Work	119
Lemonade	82
Mock	82
Portable	83
Light Gingerbread	100
Liver, Fried	30
Dried	45
Liquid Polish	142
Loaf Cinnamon	50
Liquid Glue	130
Macaroni	39
Marmalade, Quince	74
Mixed	74
Marble Mantles, Cleansed	109
Manuscripts Renovated	113
Mangoes, Pickled	41
Martinoes, Pickled	40
Meat, Pudding under	26
Measures	49

	PAGE
Mitten, Wash	135
Medals, to take Impress of	120
Meringue, Apple	61
Moths	115
Mush	12, 86
Cakes	12
Mutton, Roast	26
Chops	30
Mufflers	133
Muffins	10
Mock Lobster	48
Mucilage	130
Needles	99
Nurse's Home	85
Nursing	85
Netting	141
Oil Cloth, Wash	109
Okra	93
Omelet, Baked	15
Tomato	16
with Cheese	17
Onions, Boil	37
Pickle	42
Oysters, Stew	47
Plant	16, 48
Fry	39
Scalloped	31
Pickled	47
Sauce	39
Orange Cocoa-nut	97
Parsnips	35
Pastry	56
Another, simpler	57
Paste for Papering	111
Painting	111
Paint, Economical	111
Panada	86
Panada, Egg	87
Barley	87
C. F. B. M	87
Chicken Water	87
Peas	35
Pepper Sauce	41
Pickle, Universal	41
India	41
Polish Boots	139
Peach Leather	75
Peaches, Spiced	43
Pickled	44
Uncooked	95
Pears	76, 151
Peaches	74, 76, 151
Picture Frames	122
Pigeons	29

INDEX.

	PAGE		PAGE
Pig, Roast	25	Quince Jam	70
Pie, Oyster	57	Quick Milk Biscuit	100
Chicken	57		
Pot	58	Raspberry Vinegar	82
Mince	58	Rabbits	29
Apple	58	Relish, A	13, 17, 46
Plaut	59	Re-pot Plants	147
Planting Seeds	146	Ribbons, to Color	110, 114
Plants, coming into Flower	148	Rice, to Boil	33
Plant, Egg	38	Pudding	61
Plums, Pickled	44	Flummery	17
Plums, Crystalized	75	Rolls, Potato	9
Pork, Pickled	44	French	10
Potatoes, Sweet	94	Roses	149
White	33, 95	Roaches, Eradicate	112
Potatoe Masher	98	Rock Work	152
Rolls	9	Raspberry Jam	80
Potochomauia	122, 127	Rachahout	92
Pot Plants	146, 147		
Preserved Limes	73	Sauce, Pepper	41
Cocoa-nut	71	Sandwiches	48
Pine Apple	71	Salmon, to Boil	20
" " grated	72	Sausage	13, 18
Common Cherries	11	Sauce, Caper	39
Gooseberries	72	Egg	39
Quinces	72	Celery	40
Citron Melon	72	1, 2, 3, 4	68
Pears	76	Salad, Chicken	46
Peaches	72, 76, 151	Scrapple	18
" Uncooked	73, 97	Sea-weed, Colored	154
Damsons	73	Seats	124
Prints, Cleaning	113	Shad, Broil	19
Pudding, Pumpkin	59	Pickled	48
Potato	59	Bake	19
Green Corn	59, 60	Boil	20
Flemish	60	Shoes, to Make	125
Save All	60	Shawl, to Net	132, 141
Cocoa-nut	60	Crochet	144
Custard	60	Silver, Cleansed	108
Soda Cracker	60	Slaw, Cold	35
Rice	61	Souse	18
Macaroon	61	Soap for Mouse-holes	107
Adelaide's	62	Soaps	101, 102, 103
Cup Batter	62	Socks, Infants'	133
Boiled Batter	62	Soup, Beef, &c	21
Bread	63	Okra	22
Delightful	63	Chicken	22
Cottage	63	Pea	22
Bird's Nest	65	Clam	22
Pudding, Tapioca	65	Vegetable	85
Baked Indian	65	Portable	23
under Meat	26	Spinach, Boil	38
Pickled Salmon	48	Spots, Take Out	114, 115
Preserved Orange Skin	97	Starch	105
Potato Biscuit	99	Stains, Take Out	108
Paste that will keep	130	Stand, Bottle	141

	PAGE		PAGE
Squirrels	29	Trifle	97
Stuffing	39	Tomato Figs.	98
Syllabub	64	Tomatoes, Preserved	99
Syrup, Vanilla	81		
Strawberry	81	Useful Implements	98
Ginger	81	Useful Work	117
Sally Lunn	9		
Salt Shad	17	Vases, Garden	152
Sour Plums Preserve	99	Verbenas	148
Sour Milk Bread	99	Vegetables, to Keep	33, 93
Sweet Potato Biscuit	100	Veal, Roast	25
Stains in Table Linen	154	Vol au Vent	58
		Veal Cutlets	28
Table Knives and Forks	99		
Table Cover to Crochet	143		
Tea	13, 86	Waffles	11
Tea, Beef	88	Quick	11
Tidy, Chair	135, 136, 141	Rest	11
Tomato, Stewed	37	Rice	11
Broiled	18	Walnuts, Pickled	42
Baked	19, 37, 38	Water, Gum	85
Stew	27	Muffins	7
Fried	38	Wall, to Paper	110
Omelet	16, 38	Wash, Camphene	109
To Keep	96	Warts, to Remove	153
Catsup	43	Weights	49
Pickled	41, 43	Weak Back	153
Tooth Paste	143	Whey, Wine	88
Tomato Mustard	43	Whitewashes	114
Tongue	47	Wine, Currant	81
Toy Scrap-book	126	Quince	81
Toys, Children's	126	Cherry	81
Transplanting	147	Winter Stores	93
Trifle	64		
Turkey, Roast	25	Yard, to Red	109
Boiled	26	Yeast	5
Turnovers, Cold Meat	31	Dry	6
Turnips	37	Hop	6

www.ingramcontent.com/pod-product-compliance
Lightning Source LLC
Chambersburg PA
CBHW030305170426
43202CB00009B/875